The Ungraded Middle School

Robert J. McCarthy

PARKER PUBLISHING COMPANY, INC.   West Nyack, N.Y.

To Kathie
--for her love and
for
her support of these ideas

© 1972 *by*

PARKER PUBLISHING COMPANY, INC.

West Nyack, N.Y.

Library of Congress
Catalog Card Number: 76-169612

Printed in the United States of America
ISBN-0-13-937326-8
B & P

ABOUT THE AUTHOR

Robert J. McCarthy is a former junior high school and middle school principal. He has had firsthand experience in reorganizing early adolescent education in both urban and suburban communities. As principal of the Liverpool Middle School, Liverpool, New York, and as the Assistant Superintendent for Instruction in Englewood, New Jersey, he planned the transition from traditional, departmentalized junior high school structures to ungraded, interdisciplinary approaches to instruction in middle schools. Mr. McCarthy has spoken at ASCD and AASA conventions on the topic of the middle school movement, has taught graduate level courses on the subject, and has served as a consultant to numerous school districts throughout the United States. He has been a high school principal and is currently the Superintendent of Schools in East Greenwich, Rhode Island.

Foreword

In this book Robert McCarthy has embodied many of the latest innovations and trends in modern education as they pertain to the early secondary school program. He most emphatically and systematically places the emphasis and merits of the Middle School concept upon the values to be derived from such an organizational structure by the learner. He focuses his writing on the flexibility such a program affords the learner and stresses the fact by utilizing the concept of the nongraded Middle School. The learner is guided toward learning for learning's sake with the eventual goal of independent study. This design and structure takes full advantage of a program constantly moving from the static to the dynamic and is always open-ended.

A most significant acknowledgement is made to the important and changing role of the Building Principal who, according to Mr. McCarthy, is responsible for the creation of the building climate and the personality of the school building. This learning environment comes about through the use of a leadership team from which the principal emerges as a true educational leader whose major responsibility is to bring together the expertise and talents of the instructional consultant, the pupil personnel consultant, and the independent study coordinator to bear upon a child's learning.

Throughout the book there is a strong emphasis upon learning and instruction as being a team function, both administratively and instructionally. *The Ungraded Middle School* dramatically spotlights the feasibility and the necessity for the establishment of a nongraded interdisciplinary structured school program. It is at this age that young people need a flexible multi-faceted program within which they have the opportunity to try out their intellectual, social, and cultural "wings" and to be free to experiment with the skills learned at lower levels. Such a program is free of the threat of failure by any child. The Middle School as portrayed by the author is a success experience for the individual child.

Robert McCarthy is well qualified to write on such an important subject as the Middle School, from a pragmatic as well as a theoretical viewpoint. He has not been just an observer on the educational scene. His credentials display experience as a teacher, Supervising Principal, High School Principal, Assistant Superindendent for Instructional Services, and School Superintendent. He has been involved in rural, suburban and city school systems. He has been called upon to convert two relatively large traditional Junior High Schools into productive, meaningful Middle Schools, (one a city school, one a suburban school). He was eminently successful in both instances and teachers and students profited.

Progress requires all forward-looking educators to keep abreast of the latest developments in the field and Robert McCarthy's book brings to the fore some of the latest and most cogent thinking on the organization and conduct of the Middle School.

Peter J. Dugan
Superintendent of Schools
Englewood, New Jersey

How This Book Can Help You . . .

This book provides it's readers—including board members—with concrete examples of how to initiate, organize, operate, and evaluate an ungraded middle school. It advocates moving to this new organizational pattern only if the age-grade levels to be served are placed in nongraded, interdisciplinary team teaching situations, with adequate opportunities for independent study for students and flexible creative use of time and facilities by staff.

This book gives detailed accounts of actual steps taken to launch ungraded middle school programs in a variety of communities. The initial success of the reorganization in one community followed by its demise is carefully analyzed and compared with sustained success achieved in other communities. The reactions of students, staff, and community to the middle school are also included in this study.

The reader will learn how a completely departmentalized, subject-matter-centered, 7-8-9 junior high school, in a very traditional building, evolved into an interdisciplinary, student-centered, 6-7-8 middle school. Key factors that had to be considered in getting teachers from the major disciplines of English, Social Studies, Science, and Mathematics to cooperate and operate successfully as a team are thoroughly explored. It is the opinion of this author that the success of the middle school lies in the composition of the team and its operational efficiency. Illustrations are given to demonstrate the methods used by members of the team to group their students, schedule them within a block of time, and develop different curriculums on a concept-oriented basis while still developing essential skills.

The practicalities of ungradedness and individualized instruction are explored on an operational as well as a theoretical basis. Examples are given to demonstrate that individualized instruction does not mean that each student has a different curricular program. This misunderstanding of the meaning of individualized instruction has caused many teachers to focus on the "mathematical impossibility" of achieving such a goal. The nongraded middle school, developed with a definite structure, allows different students at a similar point in learning, regardless of their age or grade, to be grouped together for instruction in certain skill or concept areas for a period of time. A pattern is thus established to allow for continual pupil progress at different, individualized rates. The factors which the interdisciplinary teams consider when grouping and regrouping their students are discussed in detail.

Many parents and teachers, as well as administrators, fear that any school labeled "nongraded" or "ungraded" must be disorganized and chaotic. This myth is destroyed by a thorough analysis of the very nature of the structure of the ungraded middle school. The author presents various organizational patterns in existence today in various middle schools, and comments on their degree of flexibility and ungradedness.

The role of the building principal and his relationships with the various student-teacher teams is graphically illustrated. Methods employed to help students and staff gain self-confidence in this new organizational pattern are presented. The importance of staff involvement is stressed, as well as the necessity for paid, in-service summer institute study prior to the opening of school. An operational timetable is presented outlining the steps to be taken to insure the project's success.

Since the key to the success of the ungraded middle school lies in the placement of each student with the appropriate interdisciplinary team of teachers, the rationale for the composition of a team is studied. Individual personality patterns and educational philosophy, as well as risk-taking factors, are shown as greatly influencing the make-up of a team. As each team begins to establish its indentity, the leadership team of the building must follow certain procedures in placing each student with his team. The entire operation is explored step-by-step as it actually took place in several middle schools.

Two new advisory positions are advocated in this publication: the Instructional Consultant and the Coordinator for Independent Study and

Student Research. While the principal traditionally has been assumed to be the educational leader of the building, an analysis of the duties and responsibilities of the instructional consultant, which are neither administrative nor supervisory in nature, may cause the reader to realize that such a nonthreatening position may well be the key to curricular development and instructional proficiency in the middle school. The role of the I.C. differs greatly from that of an assistant principal, and the author also advocates the elimination of the assistant principalship at the middle school level.

The coordinator of Independent Study and Student Research helps teachers and teams identify students capable and desirous of pursuing learning outside the confines of the typical classroom. The rationale for this position in the middle school, as well as the producures followed in initiating the program, are explored. The duties and responsibilities of the coordinator are outlined and examples are given of the various forms developed to help students become independent learners. A unique evaluation procedure wherein the student, his teacher, and the coordinator evaluate the work undertaken is discussed in detail.

Additional chapters deal with the various curricula appropriate for middle school students, initiating ungraded programs in both modern and traditional physical plants, and with the new role that guidance counselors must play in working with students and teaching teams. All examples cited have been operational with varying degrees of success in several middle schools.

This book will not only provide a sound basis for the ungraded middle school, but a model to choose from in planning an organizational structure. Examples and plans are cited and, if followed with adaptions geared to the local school-community setting, will help insure the success of the ungraded middle school.

Robert J. McCarthy

Contents

Rationale for the middle school. The middle school de-fined. How it differs from the junior high. Preparing staff for the shift to a middle school. Selecting the consultant and the consulting team. Phase I: general overview. Phase II: intensive staff workshop. Phase III: the summer orientation program. Phase IV: follow-up seminar. Preparation of parents and pupils.

The basis for reorganization. Why graded?. Ungraded-ness—a flexibility necessity. The leadership team concept. Teaching teams. Advantages of teaming.

Curriculum defined. Curricular goals. Recommended course offerings. Interdisciplinary Unit #1—the sea around

mances. Keeping apprised of instructional programs. The principal's role in disciplinary matters. Other job demands.

Relationships with teachers and teams. Assigning students to teams. Counselors must visit classrooms. Attendance at team planning sessions. Reporting pupil progress. Errors to be avoided in reporting. High school preparation.

A Teacher's View of Interdisciplinary Teaming by Eric Martinsen. A Coordinator's Observations on Independent Study by Vincent Hemmer. A Guidance Program for Early Adolescents by Albert Cappalli. Observations of an Instructional Consultant by Raymond F. Stopper, Jr. The Role of the Middle School Principal by Peter Telfer, Jr.

Chapter 1

Launching An Ungraded
Middle School

SCHOOL DISTRICTS ACROSS the nation are in the process of analyzing their grade-level housing patterns. Reasons advanced for such studies are: to comply with court rulings on the segregation-integration controversy; to alleviate overcrowded conditions at either the elementary or secondary levels; to alter existing grade-level arrangements to better suit today's youth; or to hop on the bandwagon of educational change.

The first reason for such organizational rearrangements is a valid one, considering the true function of the educational process. The second reason may be a very realistic one in terms of the present school housing crisis in many urban and suburban communities. The basic intent of this chapter, however, is to focus on what should be the rationale underlying the middle school movement, namely, the needs of today's early adolescents.

The youth this organizational change will affect, the influences it should have on teaching and administrative personnel, and the preparations that must be undertaken if the transition is to be successful are also analyzed in detail.

Rationale for the Middle School

For many reasons today's youth are far different from the youth of previous generations. It has been pointed out that the present school population has been brought up in an electronic and technical environment, virtually non-existent for their parents when young. One of Marshall McLuhan's theses is that this new environment for learning, with its shift from a literary to an oral oriented culture, has created numerous problems for those of previous generations nutured by books rather than by television.[1] Today's students see and become emotionally involved in sights and events never viewed before: a walk on the moon, a teachers' strike, an ongoing war, and the clash of youth with police. It is difficult to comprehend the effects that these events and impressions must have on our school age populations.

Aside from these environmental changes, our society has now become an extremely mobile one. Skills once thought to be essential for employment are obsolete before they are mastered. With these shifting conditions students have been forced to adjust in many ways.

Tanner in his studies of maturation has noted one such adjustment to these changes in the environment. He states that

> During the last 100 years there has been a very striking tendency for the time of adolescence, as typified by menarche or the growth spurt, to become earlier. The data on heights and weights of children of school age and before show that the whole process of growth has been progressively speeded up and that at all ages children born in the 1930s or 1950s, for example, were considerably larger than those born in the 1900s.[2]

These physical changes, combined with parental pressures for early dating and college admissions, reinforced by the commercial push for cosmetics and slightly padded bras, have a pronounced effect on the youth of today, forcing early adolescents to face maturity at an earlier age.

Junior high schools were created in the early 1900s in response to the physical, intellectual, emotional, and social needs of the early adolescents of that day; and since many of these conditions have been drastically altered within the past fifty or sixty years, it seems reasonable to assume that it might be profitable to examine the existing junior high school structure to see if it is appropriate for today's young adolescents.

Today's departmentalized, subject matter oriented junior high schools, with their large enrollments, students shifting every 42 or 45 minutes from teacher to teacher, and their rigid grade and grouping practices, have been frequently criticized for failing to meet the needs of the students they were supposed to serve. They in practice have become what they were not intended to be, mirror images of their high schools.

---

1. Marshall McLuhan, *Understanding Media: The Extensions of Man* (New York: McGraw-Hill Book Co. 1964).

2. J. M. Tanner, *Growth at Adolescence* (Oxford: Blackwell Scientific Publications, 1962), p. 143.

As Gruhn and Douglass have pointed out, "the junior high school today still fails to meet satisfactorily the needs, abilities, and interests of individual boys and girls."[3] Numerous reasons have been advanced for this failure to achieve the educational goals established when the junior high schools were first initiated. Perhaps it can be traced to weaknesses in the administrative structure of the design, or to the thesis advanced by Alvin Howard that "the conditions which originally gave impetus to the junior high movement either no longer exist or are considerably changed."[4]

This last hypothesis bears further scrutiny. If one reads Dacus' doctoral dissertation[5] dealing with various aspects of maturity and the graded organizational structure of the junior high school, it reveals that sixth and seventh grade pupils are, in general, quite similar. It also indicates that ninth and tenth grade students are similar in many ways. Rowe also states that

> Physicians, psychologists and physiologists report that children mature at a rate of four to twelve months faster than they did 40 years ago. And it appears obvious that children are becoming more socially sophisticated at an earlier age than they did in the past.[6]

These findings, along with Tanner's studies on physical growth, would seem to indicate that a new organizational structure needs to be created for today's early adolescents.

This new institution would house students who have similar physical, emotional, social, and intellectual needs. If sixth graders are more similar to seventh graders today, and if ninth graders are more similar to tenth graders today than they were forty or fifty years ago when junior high schools were first being established, then it would seem most logical to have senior high schools housing ninth grade along with the tenth, eleventh, and twelfth grades, and the intermediate or middle schools housing grades six, seven, and eight.

The previously mentioned studies have shown how today's sixth, seventh, and eighth grade students are different from those of other eras. Since they are different, the school must develop new educational goals for them, explore new curricular offerings, reexamine old methods of instruction and initiate new ones, and establish new internal structures within these middle schools to meet the needs of the students.

---

3. William T. Gruhn and Harl R. Douglas, *The Modern Junior High School* (New York: The Ronald Press Company, 1947), p. 248.

4. Alvin Wendell Howard, *The Middle School in Oregon and Washington 1965-1966* (Doctoral dissertation, University of Oregon, 1966), p. 3.

5. Wilfred P. Dacus, *A Study of the Grade Organizational Structure of the Junior High School as Measured by Social Maturity, Emotional Maturity, Physical Maturity, and Opposite-Sex Choices* (Doctoral dissertation, University of Houston, 1963).

6. Robert N. Rowe, "Why We Abandoned Our Traditional Junior High," *Nation's Schools*, January, 1967, p. 74.

To shift from a 7-8-9 junior high school organizational pattern to a 6-7-8 middle school arrangement, with no corresponding internal restructuring of the educational program, is to do nothing at all. Unfortunately this is occurring much too frequently today with the result that most middle school programs are, in reality, little more than junior high programs moved down one or two grades.

Since today's ninth grade students have greater and different curricular needs than their younger and less mature junior high counterparts, and since they also appear in many ways to be intellectually and socially alienated from these seventh and eighth grade students, many districts are returning to the four-year, 9-12, high school. The earlier maturation and increased sophistication of today's youth also leads to the conclusion that the majority of elementary schools cannot adequately meet the demands of the current sixth grade population. These youngsters want to explore the areas of industrial arts, home economics, science lab, music, art, foreign languages, and physical education on a regular, daily basis. They also need to be exposed to teachers who have more expertise in a particular discipline than is common among most elementary trained teachers. These factors, combined with the needs of sixth grade students to use the far more adequate facilities of secondary school library resource centers, have convinced some districts to establish 6-7-8 middle schools.

The Middle School Defined

The middle school is that educational institution encompassing children ordinarily included in grades six, seven, and eight, that is specifically designed in its operations to meet the needs of early adolescents. Some schools which house grades five through eight are also called middle schools.

Although the assignment of age-grade levels to buildings is of vital concern to the school district, it is what actually goes on within that physical plant that will determine the success or failure of the undertaking.

There are however definite advantages to a 6-7-8 middle school as opposed to a 5-6-7-8 school. In middle schools which include the fifth grade in their organizational structure, there is a tendency for the community and the professional staff to treat the sixth graders like elementary pupils. With such an arrangement the fifth and sixth grades are usually organized on a self-contained basis while the seventh and eighth grades are mainly departmentalized. This means that this type of middle school has merely copied, lock, stock, and barrel, the fifth and sixth grade operations as they existed in the elementary school, and the seventh and eighth grade structure as it existed in the junior high school, and done nothing else. This internal division of the school, along purely arbitrary grade-level lines is establishing a rigidity that is the antithesis of the flexibility desirable in middle schools.

A middle school must, if it is to achieve its goals of developing educational programs well suited to early adolescents, establish an organizational structure that is appropriate for these youngsters. This requires combining the basic concern of the elementary school for the "whole" child with the traditional emphasis of the secondary school on subject matter mastery. The synthesis should result in the establishment of an educational institution that will better serve youngsters in the 10 through 13 age bracket.

How It Differs from the Junior High

While many lofty goals were put forth when the junior high schools were first created, in essence the very phrase "junior high" forecast that it would ultimately become a watered down high school for younger students. Rather than taking the children from where they were in their educational progression as they left the elementary school and having the freedom to develop appropriate curricular programs in an attempt to individualize instruction, the school was regarded as merely a preparation for high school. This naturally imposed tremendous restrictions on the teaching and administrative personnel associated with the junior high in terms of Carnegie units, specific course content to be covered, and a fixed number of minutes of classroom instruction in each course each semester.

The notion of the junior high as preparation for high school even applies to teachers who are often required to serve an apprenticeship in the junior high before being assigned to the high school position they seek. Few colleges prepare teachers for working with youngsters in so-called junior high schools. Thus pupils in these schools are not educated in terms of their own need to learn at this specific point in their lives.

It must be understood from the start that the middle school is *not* intended to serve merely as a transitional institution to "bridge the gap" between the self-contained structure of the elementary school and the totally departmentalized structure of the typical secondary school. The middle school's main objective is to develop those educational programs that will allow each individual student to make continuous progress in learning. To achieve this goal, somewhat the same one as originally set for the junior high school, there must be some radical departures from previous teaching, administrative, and organizational patterns prevalent at the secondary level. This can perhaps best be summarized by a chart, Figure 1-A, comparing the traditional junior high school arrangement with that of a middle school specifically designed for modern early adolescents.

Middle School	*Junior High School*
1. Grades 6-7-8.	1. Grades 7-8-9.
2. Exploratory curriculum.	2. Curriculum is predetermined.
3. Purpose is to prepare for continuous learning.	3. Purpose is to prepare for high school.
4. Interdisciplinary teaming approach to instruction.	4. Departmental organization prevails.
5. Key decisions on grouping and scheduling made by teaching staff.	5. Key decisions on grouping and scheduling made by administrators and guidance counselors.
6. Individualized instruction.	6. More fixed teaching and grouping practices.
7. Teams of teachers focus on individual student needs and interests.	7. Individual teachers focus on subject matter mastery.
8. Modular scheduling varying daily.	8. 42 or 45 minute classes each day.
9. Flexibility prevails.	9. Rigidity prevails.
10. Increased opportunities for independent study.	10. Limited opportunity for independent study.

Figure 1-A
Comparison of Middle with Junior High Schools

Although the organization of a school in itself cannot guarantee successful education, it is indispensable for implementing the desired educational programs. It will be classified as an effective organizational pattern if it provides the basic framework within which the stated educational objectives of the institution can be achieved, an ineffective one if it does not. But this basic pattern must be geared to the needs of the children concerned, and not just for the convenience of the administration. The junior high pattern was and is very convenient for administrators and teachers, but it is no longer appropriate for today's students.

The junior high school was initially created because of a need. It was hoped that its structure would serve its students. It did for a time, but then the organizational structure began to determine the activities of the school. When the need for new educational activities arose, demanding new organizational patterns, the junior high schools were either unable or unwilling to adapt to the changing times. An organization to be successful must be flexible and dynamic, not fixed and static. The junior high shool represents the status quo, while the middle school offers the hope of a flexible, newly created, dynamic structure, designed to serve its students.

Therefore if the middle school is to achieve its goals, it must, in this author's opinion, be:

1. A nongraded school, in which
2. Interdisciplinary teaming must prevail, and where
3. Many opportunities are present for initiating independent study programs.

In addition to this,

A. Teachers must have responsibility for grouping and scheduling their students.
B. The curriculum must be extremely flexible.
C. Different methods of reporting pupil progress to parents from those commonly used on the secondary level must be developed.
D. Teams of students and teams of teachers should be associated with each other for a span of at least two years.

Since the 6-7-8 middle school organized along these lines is so vastly different from the previously existing junior high schools, adequate preparation for the transition must be provided for the teaching and administrative staffs, the students, and the community.

Preparing Staff for the Shift to a Middle School

Once the decision has been made by the superintendent of schools and the board of education to create a middle school or a series of middle schools within the district, a plan must be developed to thoroughly orient all those involved in the shift. Before the final decision is reached, representatives of various segments of the school community, as well as teachers and administrators, should be involved in a series of discussions about the contemplated move.

Although it is taken for granted that the leadership team of the district has definite reasons for creating a middle school, and also has some very definite goals in mind for this new organizational structure, it cannot be assumed that the rest of the district's professional staff will have similar understandings. Therefore it is essential that the district sponsor a lengthy, well organized in-service orientation program that will sufficiently prepare all those involved in this undertaking for the change. This program should begin at least one year, if not two, prior to the opening of the district's first middle school. Such preparation is so important that no district should attempt such a transition to a middle school without a thorough orientation program.

This program should include four distinct phases that are specifically designed to thoroughly prepare the entire professional staff for the new roles they are to play. The four-phase program that, in this author's professional judgment, is essential for the success of the middle school is as follows:

I. A general overview of the middle school program. This should be a one-day orientation program for all intermediate and junior high school teachers, administrators, and guidance counselors, plus central office personnel. It could be held on the school district's professional day while other in-service programs are being conducted for the rest of the district.

II. A two-day intensive workshop with the staff that has been selected to work in the middle school. This should be held during the spring prior to the opening of the middle school.

III. A summer workshop for the entire middle school staff. Ideally this should be a four-week program, but it should never be less than one week, no matter what the district's financial circumstances. The type of program to be developed during this phase of the orientation will depend on the length of the summer workshop. Teachers however *must be paid* on a pro-rated basis based on their regular salary for the year if positive results are to be expected.

IV. A follow-up seminar midway through the first year of the middle school's operation. This will give the staff an opportunity to assess gains made and focus on problems encountered.

Selecting the Consultant and the Consulting Team

The chief school administrator, due to his tremendous responsibilities, cannot be expected to adequately run such an intensive and prolonged orientation program. He should delegate this responsibility to one of his central office staff. This should be either the assistant superintendent for instruction or the director of secondary education, depending on the size of the district. In systems where there will be several middle schools launched simultaneously, a three-man team consisting of the assistant superintendent for instruction, the director of secondary education, and the director of elementary education ordinarily assumes responsibility for the overall planning of the orientation program.

Since the district will be initiating a middle school program, it cannot be expected that within the system itself there will be sufficient experienced, knowledgeable personnel available to fully supervise and coordinate the orientation. The assistant superintendent and the directors, who already have other duties and responsibilities to fulfill, should therefore seek the services of an experienced consultant or consulting team to work closely with the district for approximately two years as it plans, initiates, and evaluates this new enterprise.

It is essential that the consultant to be employed by the district have had direct experience in a middle school as an administrator or a teacher. The consultant selected must be able to draw from practical experience if he or she is to work successfully with staff. There can be no substitute for this experience.

A district looking to secure the services of a well qualified, experienced middle school consultant had best be leery of employing individuals whose only connection with the middle school movement is at the theoretical level. There are professors of education who are concentrating on the middle school and early adolescent education. Much of the knowledgeable theory that they can bring to bear on the instructional approaches to be employed in the middle school is very valuable. They can most definitely be used as a resource, a possible keynote speaker, or as a member of a consulting team, but certainly not as the chief consultant since they lack the practical firsthand experience that teachers respect.

Recently a number of consulting firms have also sprung up across the country dealing with a variety of topics such as professional negotiations, programmed budgeting, flexible modular scheduling, independent study, team teaching, and the middle school. Here again discretion must be exercised. Only if the personnel employed by the consulting firm have direct working experience with a middle school should the district consider entering into a contract with them to supervise the orientation.

As was previously indicated, there are schools across the country that purport to be middle schools serving the needs of early adolescents, but many are either watered-down, glorified, departmentalized junior high schools or self-contained elementary operations. It is vitally important that a school system already have in mind what it wants its middle school to be before it selects a consultant. In this way the district can select an individual as a consultant who already agrees with its stated educational philosophy for this new instructional unit. The district can thus select the best man to fit the role.

Probably the best way to select a chief consultant for a district is to contact a professional association such as the American Association of School Administrators or the Association for Supervision and Curriculum Development. These outstanding educational organizations sponsor many workshops throughout the United States and include in their membership individuals who have assumed leadership roles in the areas of curriculum development, innovative instructional practices, and individualized organizational structures. The directors of these associations are familiar with those districts and individuals who are developing interesting programs for early adolescents and attempting to initiate nongraded, individualized approaches to education at the secondary level.

Once a consultant has been suggested, the assistant superintendent should read what that consultant has written, learn about his practical experience with the middle school movement, and determine how successful the individual has been in other consulting assignments by contacting those districts. When this has been done and the leadership team responsible for the orientation has decided that the consultant recommended is suitable, contact should be made with the consultant to determine his availability and his consulting fee. Individual consulting fees generally range from $100.00 to $150.00 per day plus expenses, depending upon background and experience. The money expended is considerable, but well worth it if the consultant selected has the credentials to do the job required of him. This is why great care must be exercised in selecting such an individual.

A weak consultant giving the initial keynote address in Phase I of the program can get the orientation off on a sour note, kill off enthusiasm, and can possibly doom the entire project to failure before it really begins. On the other hand, the right selection can give impetus to the undertaking, encouraging all concerned to put forth maximum effort to achieve the desired goals.

Phase I: General Overview

As soon as the consultant has been selected arrangements should be made to have him visit the district in the fall of the year preceding the opening of the middle school. It is suggested that this initial meeting coincide with the district's professional day ordinarily scheduled for this time of the year. The representative of the district who has been in contact with the consultant in writing and by means of telephone conversations, should inform him of the composition of the audience he will have, possible questions to be raised by members of the staff, and the overall educational, fiscal, political and social status of the district at that time.

Having received all of this information, and having asked certain questions of the district contact, the consultant must now plan an action-packed one-day workshop that will give the audience, composed of potential, and perhaps already selected, middle school administrators, counselors, and teachers, a total view of the possible directions that the middle school can take. The consultant, knowing what philosophical and educational goals the district wishes the middle school to achieve, can develop definite concrete models from his previous experience to help staff see how these goals can be reached.

The consultant generally makes his own travel arrangements, but the district should arrange for hotel or motel accommodations, someone to greet him at the airport or depot, and a host for his stay in the district. The district will of course bear all expenses incurred by the consultant for travel and meals. Arrangements must also be made to have the consultant meet with the leadership team of the district and other supervisory personnel directly concerned with the project, on the evening prior to the professional day to straighten away last minute details. The team may be able to give the consultant some last minute information that might prove to be vital to the workshop on the following day. The consultant should also be briefed on details of local color and amusing anecdotes which he can use to put his audience at ease and thus get this first session off on the right foot.

A suggested schedule to be followed for the one-day initial orientation session is outlined in Figure 1-B. The consultant's presentation should never be read, but should be crisp, lively, and highlighted with appropriate audio-visual materials that illustrate the points being developed. His remarks should serve as a stimulus for eliciting clarifying questions from the staff. Therefore it is essential that there be a question and answer period following immediately after each presentation to allow the professional staff to actively explore some of the ideas just mentioned. The consultant must answer questions raised by citing specific examples from his middle school experience if he is to develop staff confidence in himself, in his philosophy of education, and in the district's new undertaking.

9:00 - 9:15	Coffee
9:15 - 9:30	Opening remarks by the superintendent of schools and the director of the orientation program, and the introduction of the keynote speaker.
9:30 - 10:15	Keynote address by the chief consultant stressing: A. The rationale for the middle school. B. How it differs from the junior high school. C. Why the middle school must be ungraded to succeed. D. What key decision-making responsibilities must be given to teachers.

              E. Why a teaming approach to instruction must be employed.

10:15 - 10:30 Question and answer period.

10:30 - 10:45 Coffee and refreshments.

10:45 - 11:30 Remarks by the keynote speaker focusing on:
- A. The conceptual approach to instruction.
- B. Interdisciplinary as opposed to departmentalized teaming.
- C. The procedures to be followed in selecting and forming teams.
- D. Block-time scheduling and the creative use of time and facilities.
- E. The new role of the building principal and the guidance counselor.

11:30 - 11:50 Question and answer period.

11:50 - 12:50 Lunch.

12:50 - 1:30 The consultant will discuss the following points with staff:
- A. Diagnosis of student needs.
- B. Developing appropriate curriculums.
- C. Elective vs. required courses of study.
- D. Independent study programs.
- E. Evaluating and reporting pupil progress.

1:30 - 2:00 Question and answer period.

2:00 - 2:30 Seminar sessions led by members of the central office staff on the topics of:
- A. Interdisciplinary teaming.
- B. Diagnosis.
- C. Block-time scheduling.
- D. Evaluating pupil progress.

2:30 - 2:40 Break.

2:40 - 3:10 Seminar sessions. Teachers now move to a second seminar group.

3:10 – 3:20 Concluding remarks by the consultant and the director of the orientation program.

Figure 1-B

Phase I—Orientation Program

When the seminar groups are operating in the afternoon the consultant is moving from group to group, sometimes serving as a catalyst and at other times as a resource individual.

At the conclusion of the professional day the consultant should meet with the personnel in charge of the orientation for their evaluation of the day. At this time he should also share with them his own observations of the workshop. From this dialogue should emerge the interim steps that will need to be taken within the district prior to Phase II of the orientation program scheduled for the following spring. It is also an excellent idea to have developed a simple survey or questionnaire to be given to staff to ascertain their views about the first orientation session. These should be anonymous responses, but hopefully they will indicate to the consultant and the leadership team the strong and weak points of the first program and the directions that future in-service workshops should take.

Those individuals charged with the supervision of the entire orientation program for the transition to the middle school unit must now meet with the staff to plan those activities that will further prepare all concerned for the change. Teachers, administrators, and counselors should be represented on a committee that maps out the in-service educational program to be completed prior to the Phase II workshop. Such activities might include:

1. Visits to other middle schools that are attempting to develop programs and organizational structures along similar educational and philosophical lines.

2. Attendance at clinics, conventions, and workshops that are specifically focusing on some of the areas that are to be part of the desired middle school program.

3. Development of a professional library and issuance of a monthly newsletter to staff, devoted to middle school problems, practices, and innovations.

4. At least one faculty meeting per month devoted to some aspect of the program to be implemented within the year.

5. Small group discussions among members of the staff as part of a kind of *creative education council* to explore all ideas that might have a positive effect upon the emerging institution.

If some or all of these suggestions are attempted, the staff should be well disposed for Phase II of the orientation.

Phase II: Intensive Staff Workshop

The second phase of the orientation program should be held in the spring of the year preceding the opening of the first middle school. At that time it is recommended that the chief consultant return to the district accompanied by his consulting team to work intensively with the staff for two days. The consulting team should consist of individuals who are currently working in or who have recently worked in middle schools.

It is strongly recommended that the team be composed of a teacher who has worked in an interdisciplinary teaming situation, a building principal, and a guidance counselor or an instructional consultant because these are the key positions in the middle school. The members of the team must be able to thoroughly explore these positions with the staff if the school is to achieve success.

It is essential that the two-day program be action-packed with the consultants and the professional staff really zeroing in on areas of mutual concern. The consultants must state their case clearly, make use of practical examples to illustrate their points, indicate potential problem areas and how they can be avoided, and answer all inquiries in a straightforward manner based upon their previous experiences in middle schools and on other consulting assignments.

Some sort of a timetable must be followed in each workshop session so that there will be a sense of accomplishment at the end of each day, and also to avoid the tendency of educational speakers to wander from the subject of their discussion. Each consulting team should however have the freedom to vary from the schedule it created, but a definite schedule must initially be established if specific goals are to be achieved.

Figures 1-C and 1-D indicate a possible format to be followed for such a two-day conference.

9:00 - 9:15	Coffee
9:15 - 9:45	A general review of the middle school by the *chief consultant*.

    1.   Rationale for the middle school.
    2.   The organizational structure of the middle school.
    3.   Graded and nongraded philosophies.

9:45 - 10:00	Question and answer period.
10:00 - 10:15	Coffee break.
10:15 - 10:45	The teacher in the middle school by the *teacher*.

    1.   Selection of personnel for teams.
    2.   Grouping and scheduling responsibilities of teams.
    3.   The interdisciplinary curricular approach.

10:45 – 11:00	Question and answer period.
11:00 – 11:30	Guidance operations in the middle school by the *counselor* or the *instructional consultant*.

    1.   The role of the guidance counselor.
    2.   The counselor and the team.
    3.   The counselor and the curriculum.

11:30–11:45   Question and answer period.
11:45–12:45   Lunch.
12:45– 1:30   Evaluation of the middle school movement by the
              chief consultant and the *building principal.*
              1.   Community preparation.
              2.   Comparison of the middle school with the junior
                   high school.
              3.   Evaluative devices and criteria employed.
1:30 – 1:45   Question and answer period.
1:45 – 2:15   Student evaluation in the middle school by the
              teacher and *guidance counselor.*
              1.   How do you measure pupil progress?
              2.   Reporting forms employed depending on philoso-
                   phy.
              3.   Parent-team conferences.
2:15 – 2:30   Question and answer period.
2:30 – 3:15   Seminar discussions:
              1.   Evaluation–*counselor.*
              2.   Guidance–*principal.*
              3.   Teaming–*teacher.*
              4.   Scheduling–*chief consultant.*
3:15 – 3:30   Concluding remarks by the chief consultant.

Figure 1-C

Phase II–First Day's Program

9:00 – 9:15   Coffee.
9:15 – 9:45   The interdisciplinary approach to individualized
               instruction by the *teacher* and the *principal.*
               1.   Why an interdisciplinary approach?
               2.   Examples of units used successfully by teams
                    with students.
               3.   What the interdisciplinary approach means for
                    the student and for the teacher.
9:45 – 10:00   Question and answer period.
10:00–10:15   Coffee break.
10:15–10:45   Scheduling and grouping practices by the *counselor*
               and the *chief consultant.*
               1.   Use of time.
               2.   Use of facilities.
               3.   Criteria for grouping.

10:45—11:00   Question and answer period.
11:00—11:30   Independent study in the middle school by the *teacher* and the *principal*.
    1.   Organization and initiation of the program.
    2.   Student selection.
    3.   Evaluation of the projects.
11:30—11:45   Question and answer period.
11:45—12:45   Lunch.
12:45 — 1:15   The role of the building principal in the middle school by the *principal* and the *chief consultant*.
    1.   Responsibilities delegated to staff.
    2.   Decisions regarding team leaders and team operations.
    3.   Hiring and recruiting practices.
1:15 — 1:30   Question and answer period.
1:30 — 2:00   Seminar discussions:
    1.   Independent study—*teacher*.
    2.   Interdisciplinary instruction—*chief consultant*.
    3.   The role of the principal—*principal*.
    4.   Grouping practices—*counselor*.
2:00 — 2:15   Break.
2:15 — 2:45   Seminar discussions:
    1.   New role for the teacher—*teacher*.
    2.   New role for the student—*counselor*.
    3.   Implications for the high school—*chief consultant*.
    4.   Exploratory curriculums—*principal*.
2:45 — 3:00   Concluding remarks by the chief consultant, the consulting team, and the director of the orientation program.

Figure 1-D
Phase II—Second Day's Program

Within one month after the completion of Phase II of the orientation program, and after analyzing the feedback received from the professional staff and the consulting team, the composition of the middle school staff should begin to take shape. This would include the deployment of all personnel hired for the following school year and the formation of the various teaching and administrative teams. As this is going on plans should also be made for Phase III of the orientation program, the summer workshop and, if possible, an experimental summer school for students and staff.

The entire middle school staff, as a basis for continuation of employment, must be required to attend this summer workshop. The length of this session will undoubtedly be influenced to a large extent by funds available for such an undertaking. Whatever its length, it should be held in the month of August, with one week off between the end of the workshop and the beginning of the regular school term. As has been stated before, it is essential for the success of the program that the staff be paid a pro-rated salary for the workshop based on the present salary agreement.

Phase III: The Summer Orientation Program

Once the middle school staff has been hired and personnel deployed in various teaming arrangements, it is essential that these newly created units have time to work together professionally prior to the opening of school. If circumstances will permit only one week for a summer workshop, a crash program must be developed by the staff and the consulting team. In such a short program the emphasis must be on allowing the team members to become acquainted with the backgrounds of the students assigned to them. This workshop should also allow the team members to create a working relationship among themselves and with other personnel in the school.

It is recommended that this concentrated, intensive workshop be held during the third week in August, and allow all teams to:

1. Become acquainted with all the youngsters assigned to their team by consulting the guidance folders of each student.

2. Meet with the guidance counselor assigned to the team.

3. Develop diagnostic materials to be used for initial grouping of pupils.

4. Establish the schedule to be followed by the team members and their students for the first week of the school year.

5. Decide upon possible curriculum areas to be initially explored and developed with students.

6. Identify those students who have need of immediate help in certain specific skill areas such as reading, etc.

At this point in the orientation program the four-man consulting team should begin to work individually, and in pairs, with different interdisciplinary teams and with the administration of the building. They should explore in depth the roles that each individual must play within the total structure of the school. Questions that are being raised and problems that are being encountered by the various teams as they begin to operate should be thoroughly aired during the week.

Two schools with which this author had direct experience both made successful use of similar one-week professional orientation programs. The

1100 pupil Englewood Middle School, with its integrated student population, was located in an urban setting adjacent to New York City. It possessed extreme wealth and poverty. The 700 pupil Liverpool Middle School located approximately fifteen minutes from Syracuse, New York, drew most of its students from a suburban, middle class setting. Both of these schools constructed in-service programs that pursued the following format:

FIRST DAY

9:00 – 10:00   Introductory remarks by the superintendent of schools, the director of the orientation program, the chief consultant, and the principal of the middle school.

10:00–10:15   Coffee break.

10:15–11:45   Interdisciplinary teams and related arts teams work out room assignments and the organization of their team planning rooms.

11:45–12:45   Lunch.

12:45 – 3:00   All teams meet in their planning rooms and begin to explore the guidance folders of each of their students.

While this is taking place the consulting team should be sitting down with the leadership team of the building to discuss at length the mechanics of the teaming operation and the supportive role that each member of the leadership team must play in helping staff to handle their recently acquired decision-making responsibilities.

SECOND DAY

8:30 – 11:30   All teams continue to meet in their planning rooms to explore the guidance folders of their students. The counselors attend these sessions to share important background information about individual students with the teams. While this is taking place the consulting team is continuing to meet with the building leadership team.

11:30–12:30   Lunch.

12:30 – 2:15   All workshop participants hear presentations by the panel of consultants on the topics of:
1. Freedom and Creativity in Developing Curricular Programs for Students Within a Team—given by the *teacher* member of the consulting team.
2. Flexible Scheduling Within the Team—by the *principal* who is a panelist.

3. Appropriate Groupings for Instruction—by the *counselor* member of the team, or by the *instructional consultant.*

4. Team Leadership—by the *chief consultant.*

2:15 — 2:30   Break

2:30 — 3:00   Question and answer period.

THIRD DAY

9:00 — 10:20   Two members of the consulting team meet with team #1 in their planning room while the other two consultants meet with team #2 in their planning room. The other teams are meeting with counselors and working on pupil folders, initial student grouping procedures, and schedules for the students and the team.

10:20–10:35   Break.

10:35–11:55   Same schedule as above except that the consultants now meet with teams #3 and #4.

11:55–12:55   Lunch.

12:55 — 2:15   Same schedule as above except that the consultants meet with teams #5 and #6.

2:15 — 3:35   Same schedule as above except that the consultants meet with teams #7 and #8.

FOURTH DAY

The schedule for the fourth day of the summer orientation program is the same as the previous day's schedule except that the pairs of consultants now meet with those teams, interdisciplinary and related arts, that they did not meet with on the third day of the workshop.

FIFTH DAY

9:00 — 12:00   Interdisciplinary and related arts teams function independently in their planning rooms and in their classrooms. The day's program is subject to alterations and modifications according to the recommendations of the building principal, his leadership team, and the staff.

12:00 — 1:00   Lunch.

1:00 — 2:00   Concluding remarks by the middle school building principal, the members of the consulting team, and the director of the orientation program.

If however a school district is fortunate enough to be able to finance a four-week summer orientation, a different program can be planned which can incorporate the services of volunteer students for two hours each day to help the teams learn how to function effectively. While the first week of the workshop session might follow a pattern similar to the one previously mentioned, the remaining three weeks of the orientation should allow the interdisciplinary and related arts teams to test some of their ideas on the students participating in the program.

Students should be randomly assigned to interdisciplinary and related arts teams, and the teams should then in turn be paired to act as critic teams for each other. While students are with one team for the two-hour period of time during the morning, the critic team should observe what is taking place. After the students leave for the day, the teaching team should itself analyze what had occurred. Then the critic team gives its analysis of what it had observed. This would hopefully lead to further analysis and discussion. The critic team should also sit in on the team planning sessions, but must share their perceptions of this activity with the other team at a later date, rather than during the planning session.

Thus the schedule for such a day might be as follows:

9:00 – 11:00   A team of teachers (A) working with a group of students while another team of teachers (B) observes and takes notes.

11:00   Students are dismissed for the day.

11:00 –12:00   Team A analyzes what took place, noting successes and failures. Team B sits in on this session.

12:00 – 1:00   Lunch.

1:00 – 2:00   Team B shares with Team A its analysis of the morning's activities.

2:00 – 3:00   Team A plans for the next day while team B observes.

After team A has worked with its students for three consecutive days, it should switch roles with team B, allowing B to work directly with these same students, while A now observes the team in action and acts as a critic. This switching of roles should prove to be an excellent learning experience for the teachers and their students. While this is going on the consultants act as resource persons and as catalysts when needed.

If the three-week session with students is to be successful, it must be a completely enjoyable period of time for these youngsters, and thus there can be no such thing as homework assignments. This should be a time when teachers truly work with students by getting to know them and their interests. This summer experience can then serve as a basis for developing varied instructional programs. It can also be an excellent opportunity for the teachers and the teams to experiment, and get their feet wet in the new operation. Since students are not threatened with tests, quizzes, and grades, it can also be a uniquely enjoyable learning experience for them.

Phase IV: Follow-up Seminar

Many districts, having developed a well organized orientation program for the professional staff, think that this is sufficient to guarantee the success of the middle school. They fail to realize that, while such an initial program is necessary, there is also a definite need for continuing with the services of the consulting team throughout the first year of the middle school's operation. The staff must be able to meet with those individuals who worked so closely with them during the year preceding the opening of the school.

The consulting team, or individual consultants, should return to the district when requested to do so by the professional staff. Thus the staff would have to indicate to its building principal the consultants that were wanted, when they were needed, and for what purposes. The consultants, once contracted by the building principal or the director of the orientation program, would return to the district where their services would be used as the needs of the staff dictated.

It is strongly recommended that no consultants return to the district until the new program has been in operation for at least two months. The staff must be given time to work things out on its own and not merely allowed to turn to others for solutions to their problems. When the consultants do return they should observe the program in operation for a day, listen to the questions posed and comments made by the teaching and administrative personnel, and then give their analysis of the situation and their professional recommendations.

This continuing educational program, employing a four-phase approach for preparing staff for a new instructional operation, should enable the middle school to start off smoothly.

Preparation of Parents and Pupils

Just as consultants were employed to orient staff to the middle school, these same resource people can also be scheduled to meet with members of the community. These meetings can coincide with the dates established for staff workshops. At this time parents can be informed as to the reasons for the creation of the middle school, how it will function, and how it will benefit their children. It is also suggested that, several months prior to the opening of the school, an open house be held. At this time the Leadership Team of the building can explain, clearly and concisely, to parents of incoming elementary school students as well as to other interested parties, just how the new program will operate. After the initial presentation, time should be provided for parents to ask questions not only of the administration but also of the teachers present. This can be followed by informal discussions over coffee, or additional meetings held in the elementary schools that feed into the new middle school, until all areas of concern are thoroughly and honestly explored.

The best possible orientation for students will be the approach that staff takes when these youngsters first enter the middle school. Hopefully some will have received an initiation to the nongraded, interdisciplinary teaming approach in the experimental summer session. If all have not had an opportunity to become involved in such a program, it is imperative that each team and each teacher in the middle school sit and talk with students about the program during the first week of the school year.

It is suggested that each team meet in large groups with all its students on the first day of school. At this time the team should explain, in simple terms, how it plans to function. The students then should have a chance to ask questions of the team. When this is done, it is recommended that each teacher meet with groups of from four to six students to begin to develop a personalized, humanized approach to the entire instructional program. These meetings should last for about ten or fifteen minutes. While this is taking place, the other students should be completing diagnostic testing materials developed by the staff. This material will give the teams further information that should influence the development of curricular programs.

These meetings, combined with parent orientation sessions at each of the elementary schools that feed into the middle school, can instill confidence in the parents. With the staff of the newly created middle school conducting such meetings throughout the district, doubts and confusion should be alleviated by a thorough discussion of the entire middle school operation.

If these procedures are followed, and parents and pupils are fully informed about all aspects of the middle school program, the chances of serious complications arising are greatly minimized.

Summary

There should be no decision to implement a six, seven, eight middle school program within a district unless the school system is willing to commit staff, time, and finances to the undertaking. The reasons for the creation of this new organizational structure, and the manner in which it will differ from the previously established junior high school must be thoroughly explained to the public and to the professional staff. There must be continuous emphasis placed on the fact that today's early adolescents are indeed different from their counterparts of thirty and forty years ago. Thus a new approach to instruction, specifically geared to young adolescents, must be initiated in an organizational framework (6-7-8) that will permit the school to meet the needs of these students.

In order to make today's educational programs relevant for middle school youth, a flexible environment must be established that will allow students and teachers to work together so that the pupils may achieve competency in various skill areas while at the same time gaining an understanding of many basic concepts vital to success in life. A non-graded, interdisciplinary team oriented school that permits youngsters to pursue independent study programs, and recognizes that many key decisions regarding the day to day operations of the building must be made by teachers rather than administrators, appears to be the organizational structure most capable of achieving these goals.

If however teachers, administrators, and guidance counselors are to be successful in meeting the increased demands placed on them in the ungraded middle school, a thorough orientation program must be initiated for all parties well in advance of the opening of the first school. The recommended four-phase orientation program should employ the services of consultants who have had direct experience in a middle school operation, and whose educational philosophy is in accord with that of the district's. The summer session and the seminars to be conducted during the first year of the middle school's operation are vital to the success of the program.

A well organized approach to the entire problem of beginning a new educational unit, combined with a series of information meetings with different groups within the community and a humanistic, personalized explanation of the operation to the students when they meet and talk with their teams of teachers, can successfully launch the ungraded middle school.

Chapter 2

The Organizational Structure of the Middle School

I F A SCHOOL is to attain its goals, it must be organized in such a way as to facilitate the attainment of its stated objectives. Once goals have been clearly established and activities have been decided upon to reach these objectives, then and only then should the organizational pattern of the institution be formulated. The framework that is ultimately decided upon should be one that supports the philosophy of the school. Since the middle school is to be a creative educational undertaking specifically designed for the benefit of early adolescents, it is to be expected that its organizational pattern will not be fixed and static—a characteristic of most junior high schools. The new middle school organizational pattern must therefore be a flexible and dynamic one. This chapter will therefore focus on the basic features of such an organizational structure and the new demands it places on principals, teachers, guidance counselors and students.

The Basis for Reorganization

Since one of the most important goals of the middle school is to help early adolescents acquire the skills necessary to become independent learners, a structure must be created that will allow this to happen. It therefore follows that the teachers of these youngsters must also be permitted to be independent operators. Since the majority of schools have their key decisions made by administrative rather than teaching personnel, a drastic change must take place in the running of the schools if this goal is to be reached.

Many of the goals set forth for middle schools were at one time advanced as reasons for erecting junior high schools. For one reason or another the junior high school failed to accomplish many of these objectives. Therefore aside from different allocations of grades per building, the middle school had best create an organizational structure different from that of the junior high if it is to avoid the pitfalls of its predecessors. It would seem that if the overall structure of the school was changed from that of the junior high, it might be much easier to implement the desired philosophy of early adolescent education.

Since the organization of a school is in reality an expression of an educational theory and philosophy, the graded, departmentalized, track oriented junior high school creates a rigid framework that tends to ignore the individual, student and teacher. Thus if the middle school is to achieve its stated objectives it must be, in this author's professional opinion, ungraded, with ample opportunities for students to pursue independent study projects, while its teachers work in interdisciplinary teams in the academic as well as the related arts areas of the curriculum.

There are those in the educational field who would argue that such a drastic change from a departmentalized, graded, lockstep junior high to an ungraded, interdisciplinary team oriented, flexible middle school must be done gradually. They would hope for a transition over a span of years, perhaps going from self-contained teams, to grade-level departmentalized teams, to multigrade departmental teams, to interdisciplinary grade-level teams, to ungraded interdisciplinary teams, and finally to a series of intensive independent study programs.

Others would argue that so many small changes over such a long period of time provide too much opportunity for the development of organized resistance, as well as causing constant, year-in-year-out readjustments for students and teachers with the ultimate goals never really coming into sight. Commenting on the psychology of human reaction to drastic versus gradual change, Farson states that

> Everyone knows how to resist small changes; they do it all the time. If, however, the change is big enough, resistance can't be mobilized against it. All change is resisted, so the question is how can the changes be made big enough so that they have a chance of succeeding.[1]

This acknowledged drastic shift to an ungraded middle school from a traditional junior high organization can be successfully completed if staff is adequately prepared for it.

---

1. Richard E. Farson, "How Could Anything That Feels So Bad Be So Good?" *Saturday Review,* September 6, 1969, pp 202-21.

Why Graded?

In order to function effectively a business corporation must have an organizational structure. Without it chaos would result.

The same need exists within a school system. The board of education and the superintendent of schools establish elementary, junior high or middle schools, and high schools within a district. They create professional and nonprofessional positions within each building and in the district office. Individuals are then hired to fill these positions and discharge the duties of their particular office. Periodically the board, upon the advice of the chief school administrator, also sets policy that determines how the staff of each building will operate.

For at least seven decades the established organizational structure in school systems has been a graded one. At the elementary level teachers were, and often still are, assigned to a particular grade level in a classroom that even has a grade label, e.g., Mrs. Doe—Grade 3—Room 3A.

The situation has not been much different at the secondary level. Here we have teachers functioning on a subject matter, grade-level basis. One finds seventh grade English teachers and tenth grade mathematics instructors. Thus the vertical pattern prevailing in most districts is a graded one from kindergarten through twelfth grade. At the elementary level there is usually a self-contained structure in existence, while at the secondary level a departmentalized program exists. But why does the graded structure continue to exist when so much information has been unearthed highly critical of this method of organization?

Two reasons account for the popularity of the grade-level organizational pattern. It is, first of all, a very easy one to administer, requiring very little thought or imagination. In addition, it has been in existence for decades. The graded pattern was developed to help handle the ever increasing numbers of students enrolling in school in the last half of the 19th century. The ungraded, one-room school eventually was forced to give way to the monitorial approach of the Lancastrian system, but even this shift was not adequate for coping with the ever increasing student population.

A very simple solution was discovered for this problem. It was decided to assign students to instructional groups according to their birthday. Thus the graded system was born in the United States.

Just as students were assigned to grades according to their age, so curriculums were also designated for particular grades. Through the years the graded system, initially created to combat the confusion surrounding the worthy principle of mass education, has become a self-perpetuating dogma in American education.

There is no reason however why this graded system should be regarded as sacrosanct. When created, little was known about individual differences. It was thought that each youngster progressed more or less like every other youngster of the same age. If this hypothesis were true, then it was appropriate for all students of the same age to be grouped together for instruction. Once together they could all pursue the same subjects in a well organized, controlled, disciplined manner.

As years passed educators gradually began to notice some of the glaring weaknesses of this system, but little headway was made in attempting to change it. The refinement of psychological testing techniques, combined with a growing awareness on the part of parents and teachers of individual student differences, raised questions concerning the appropriateness of the graded organizational structure and its implications for the student and his teacher.

The graded school resulted in fixed grade level expectations, graded textbooks, graded curriculums, graded teachers, and graded students. These so-called norms had little basis in reality. Such a system nonetheless advocated that:

1. At each grade level there are specific skills and concepts that should be learned by each student.

2. Students classified as slow or as less academically talented than others will profit if they are not promoted to the next grade. The retention at grade level will enable them to master the curriculum.

3. The students must learn to adjust to the standards established by the school and their teachers.

4. If all students are promoted to the next grade, regardless of their academic proficiency, the overall standards of the school will be lowered and all will sufffer.

Once it was realized that gradedness led to a lock-step approach to education inappropriate for many students, plans began to develop that would hopefully improve the quality of education. Beginning with the assumption that individual students are indeed different from each other and thus require different types and qualities of instruction, the idea of a school organized along lines other than graded emerged.

It must however be anticipated that the move from a graded to an ungraded organizational pattern will not take place without a struggle. A nongraded pattern will make new demands of teachers, students, parents, and administrators, many of whom will resist such changes.

Ungradedness—A Flexibility Necessity

The basic educational philosophy of the ungraded school recognizes the individuality of each student and attempts to develop policies and procedures that will permit each student to make continuous progress. In a nongraded middle school each student is taught as an individual. The student is grouped with other pupils for specific instructional purposes irrespective of his age-grade level. Each student is then permitted to progress through school and the appropriate curriculums as far and as fast as he can.

A nongraded or ungraded school is therefore defined as that educational institution whose organizational structure allows each child to progress through differentiated curricular programs at his individual rate of progress. The growth of the student is measured and evaluated in terms of the individual's own unique characteristics rather than merely in terms of group grade-level standards. This is a radical departure from the graded structure which is tailored to the mythical "average" student and in which the needs of the individual pupil are frequently subordinated to the needs of the group.

If we acknowledge the fact that children have different physical, emotional, social, psychological, and intellectual needs; that they grow at different rates and learn at different speeds; and if we believe that students achieve better when they meet with success rather than failure, then the absurdity of the graded structure with all of its implications becomes eminently clear. It has only been within the confines of a school that youngsters have been so divided. Such an arrangement is contrary to the real world in which they live, work, and play.

An ungraded organizational structure is needed today to help promote continuous pupil progress. Teachers must be free to group students as they wish for valid reasons, regardless of their age. This is especially true for middle schools where, as Murphy has pointed out

> Boys and girls from 10 to 14 or so exhibit a social, physical, psychological, and intellectual range that bursts the confines of grade patterns and of plain chronology. What they need above all is to be treated and taught as individuals.[2]

The freedom to group students as situations dictate has been severely limited by barriers created by the graded organizational pattern.

Ungradedness thus brings to the school that flexibility which is necessary for the development of individualized student programs. It destroys the rigid grade-level framework previously in existence. It shatters many age-old beliefs: that there is a definite classroom environment that must prevail everywhere; and that there is a definite, prescribed curriculum for every age and its corresponding grade.

---

2. Judith Murphy, *Middle Schools* (New York: Educational Facilities Laboratories, Inc., 1965), p. 11.

A study conducted by Cook and Clymer highlights the need to provide for individual differences. They point out that

> When intelligence is measured and converted to age units, the range among first-graders (6-year-olds) is 4 years. At the seventh-grade level (12-year-olds) the range is 8 years. The typical range of ability in any grade (disregarding 2 per cent of the pupils at each end of the distribution) is equal to two-thirds of the chronological age of the median pupil in that grade.[3]

Alexander also supports these findings and indicates their significance for young adolescents.

> The range among the first graders who will enter your schools this September will be about four years. Actually in a random population 96 out of 100 children will vary from 4 to 8 years mentally, with 2 below 4, and 2 above 8. We also know that this range of ability will widen as they continue in school so that by the time these children have reached the 8th grade, you may expect a range of from 9 to 10 years in their ability. We also know that similar differences are found in their achievement in the various subjects. By the 7th grade, we can confidently expect a range between individuals of some 8 years in their achievement in the different subject fields. Furthermore, the range of achievement in various subjects by the same individual also may be great. To the extent that the range of intellectual differences among children is an argument for nongradedness (and it is the main argument, of course), there is much more basis for nongradedness in the middle years than in the primary ones.[4]

To enable youngsters to continually progress an ungraded structure must prevail, destroying the artificial grade-level barriers to possible growth. The notion that the curriculum consists of prescribed subject matter areas to be covered by all students in a particular grade cannot exist in a school system philosophically committed to the individualization of instruction. The ungraded philosophy realizes that, since each student is a unique human being, he can profit best from an educational program specifically designed for him. It further recognizes that different students must be allowed to complete courses of study in a manner and pace consistent with their own strengths and weaknesses.

The philosophical and operational differences between the two organizational patterns can perhaps best be seen by examining Figure 2-A.

But in order to organize a school on a nongraded basis, the leadership team of the building, consisting of a principal, an instructional consultant, and a pupil personnel consultant, must work closely with the rest of the

---

3. Walter W. Cook and Theodore Clymer, "Acceleration and Retardation," in *Individualized Instruction, The Sixty-first Yearbook of the National Society for the Study of Education,* Vol. I, ed. Nelson B. Henry (Chicago, Illinois: University of Chicago Press, 1962), p. 206.

4. William M. Alexander, "Program and Organization of a Five Through Eight Middle School," in *The Middle School,* ed. Thomas E. Curtis (Albany, New York: Center for Curriculum Research and Services, State University of New York at Albany, 1968), pp. 77-78.

professional staff. They must help both the interdisciplinary and related arts teams to adjust to the new structure and help them to function effectively with their newly acquired decision-making responsibilities.

Graded Structure	*Ungraded Structure*
1. Focuses on the group.	1. Emphasis is on the individual.
2. Based on the assumption that children of the same age develop in similar patterns and have similar needs.	2. Assumes that each pupil has his own unique developmental pattern and thus has different needs.
3. Prescribed curriculum with fixed standards of achievement.	3. Flexible curriculum with differentiated goals.
4. One grade-level textbook.	4. Multitext and multisensory approaches to instruction.
5. Grouping pattern is fixed.	5. Grouping patterns are constantly changing.
6. Limited opportunity for independent study.	6. Ample opportunity for students to pursue independent study.
7. Teacher–subject matter oriented.	7. Student centered.
8. If a student fails a course or series of courses, he repeats the grade.	8. Students may fail to accomplish certain goals, but they never repeat a grade.

Figure 2-A
Comparison of Graded and Ungraded Structures in Middle Schools

The Leadership Team Concept

In the past, when the primary responsibilities of the building principal were thought to revolve around scheduling students and teachers, handling discipline matters, and maintaining a good public image, the job could be handled by one individual. If the building principal was inept, the assistant principal could, and often did, do the work. In many junior high schools department chairmen assigned teachers to various classes within their department. The chairmen usually performed any tasks assigned to them by the building principal, but seldom assumed supervisory responsibilities. The teachers in such a situation only felt responsible for their own subject matter area and their own classes. The student was at the mercy of the system, occupying a low priority position in the organizational scheme.

When a school is moving from a graded junior high school to a nongraded middle school structure; when it is shifting from a departmentalized to a interdisciplinary approach to instruction; when it is creating teaching teams to replace the isolated classroom teacher pattern; when it is attempting to encourage students to pursue independent study projects, the principal alone cannot hope to be able to handle all these tasks. He must do what industry has done to cope with such a situation. He must develop a leadership team that can work as a well organized unit, each member having a specific proficiency or expertise that contributes to the overall strength of the team.

The leadership team must be composed of individuals responsible for:

1. Helping staff develop appropriate curricular programs for students,
2. Guiding pupils through this period of early adolescence,
3. Launching and coordinating independent study programs, and
4. Deploying staff, supervising personnel, developing budgets, and assuming total accountability for whatever transpires within the school.

For these reasons the leadership team of a middle school should be composed of:

1. An Instructional Consultant.
2. A Pupil Personnel Consultant.
3. A Coordinator of Independent Study and Student Research.
4. A Building Principal.

Because of the nature of the middle school program, its educational as well as its operational philosophy, there is never a need for an assistant principal, because the other members of the leadership team, as well as other staff members, assist the principal in discharging the duties of his office.

While the specific duties and responsibilities of each of the members of the building leadership team will be thoroughly explored in subsequent chapters, it might be appropriate at this point to indicate briefly how essential these four positions are to the success of the middle school by mentioning briefly their spheres of influence.

On the leadership team, the Instructional Consultant serves as a nonsupervisory counselor and helper of teachers and teaching teams. He works with the members of the professional staff in helping them to diagnose student needs and develop appropriate curricular programs for students. He must be a master teacher, sensitive to the needs of others, and capable of working with all members of the staff in a positive, hopefully nonthreatening, manner.

The Pupil Personnel Consultant is responsible for the school's guidance and pupil personnel services program. This individual must see to it that the counselors meet regularly with the different teaching teams to discuss students and to be informed of the various instructional programs being offered. Contact with parents is primarily maintained through this office. The consultant also sees to it that specific guidance counselors are assigned to specific students and specific teams for definite reasons. As the instructional consultant is to the teachers, the pupil personnel consultant is to the students.

With the staff being asked to continually evaluate student progress and to begin to operate in a teaming fashion, it would be too much to ask individual teachers to assume responsibility for different students in the area of independent study. If the school agrees that one of its primary functions is to help create independent learners, then, in attempting to encourage students and teachers to pursue such a course of action, a member of the staff must be selected to initiate and coordinate all efforts in this area. He would work in an advisory capacity with students engaged in independent research projects, while keeping individual teachers apprised of the youngsters' progress. The Coordinator of Independent Study and Student Research would also help to coordinate the evaluation procedures essential to the program.

The building principal, the fourth member of the leadership team, determines the course that the middle school will follow. The manner in which he fills this key position must be in keeping with the school's educational philosophy. Therefore it is essential that the middle school principal delegate many responsibilities to his teaching teams and to the other members of the building leadership team, that he formerly reserved for himself. The principal then serves as a catalyst and a consultant for change by creating an environment within which members of the professional staff have the opportunity to make those decisions that directly affect their operations in the building. Thus the building principal becomes the educational leader of the school to the extent that he recognizes the staff's key role in the decision-making processes that influence the instructional program. Once he recognizes this, the principal then helps his teachers to assume these new responsibilities.

Teaching Teams

Just as the school, if it is to function effectively, needs a building leadership team, so the professional teaching staff, if it is expected to approach maximum efficiency, must be organized into teaching teams. This is based on the premise that students will gain more from school if they are instructed by teams of teachers possessing different strengths and empowered with certain decision-making responsibilities, than if they are taught by individual teachers working completely independent of each other within the confines of a rigid master schedule.

A *teaching team* simply means that two or more teachers work together with students for a period of time. This broad definition can include many teaming possibilities such as:

    I. Grade-level teams;
   II. Subject matter teams;
 III. Interdisciplinary teams; and
 IV. Related Arts teams.

Since, in this author's professional opinion, an effective middle school must be nongraded, for reasons previously mentioned, and organized on an interdisciplinary teaming basis, the first two types of teams, with their obvious restrictions and limitations, will not be discussed.

An *interdisciplinary team* is defined as a team of English, Social Studies, Mathematics, and Science teachers who are given complete responsibility for planning the instructional program within these disciplines for a common body of students. While it does create the possibility for initiating interrelated curricular programs, it is basically an organizational device that presents teachers with an opportunity to improve the quality of their performance, and thus creates a better learning environment for their students.

A *related arts team* is defined as a team composed of representatives of the areas of industrial arts, home economics, music, art, and physical education, who are also given complete responsibility for planning the instructional program within and among these disciplines for a common body of students. The basic difference in operational philosophy at the middle school level between an interdisciplinary team and a related arts team is that in the latter teaming situation, students may elect not to pursue certain related arts subjects, while all pupils must take programs in the areas of English, Social Studies, Mathematics, and Science.

Advantages of Teaming

For any new organizational structure to gain acceptance, those to be affected by such a change must be made aware of the advantages of the new arrangement. The benefits of a nongraded middle school that has both interdisciplinary and related arts teams should include some of the following:

    1.   Teachers make more decisions regarding the use of their time, facilities, and curricular materials.

2. Individual students can be allowed to pursue independent study projects without disrupting the operations of the school or their classmates.

3. Teams can develop their own flexible schedules that can change daily, if necessary.

4. Grouping of students for instructional purposes is made easier because all members of the team have a common body of students which is sufficiently large and heterogeneous enough in age and ability to allow various appropriate subgroups to be formed.

5. When a member of a team is absent, the team can be of great assistance to the substitute teacher in continuing the education of the students.

6. There are increased opportunities for teachers to get to know their students and to exchange information about them.

7. Teachers on a team serve as a stimulus for each other and can help to bring about much needed curricular revisions.

8. It will attract other highly motivated teachers to the school, thus easing recruitment problems, and enabling the school to develop a top-flight staff over a period of years.

9. New teachers can learn many tricks of the trade from the more experienced team members, thus alleviating much confusion at the start of the year.

10. It gives teachers a better opportunity to individualize and personalize their instruction.

It must be realized that a teaming approach to instruction will not instantly solve all problems. Some teachers will criticize this organizational structure since it will require more of each member of the professional staff than has been asked of him in the past. The fact that all the answers are not known about the eventual outcomes of teaming will also be pointed out by some as a drawback.

In essence, the philosophical and educational orientation of the individual teacher will have much to do with the way he initially views such new working conditions. If the individual teacher has self-confidence and a genuine desire to play a more active role in the running of the school, the teaming approach has no disadvantages, only problems that need to be solved if the structure is to be totally successful.

Summary

Two of the biggest problems persistent throughout the past fifty years in education have been the inconsistency between a school's educational goals and its organizational pattern, coupled with the centralized decision-making powers of the building principal. If schools are to be run for the benefit of students, then a total reorganization has to occur that helps to remove these two roadblocks from the educational scene.

In this chapter it has been demonstrated that, if the goal of the school is to individualize instruction to enable students to become independent learners, then there is no logical basis for the existence of a school operating on a graded basis. A nongraded organizational pattern is consistent with the philosophy of continuous progress and individualized instruction whereas the graded structure is not.

The concept of the leadership team as well as that of the teaching team is based on the premise that decision-making responsibilities must reside as closely as possible with those individuals who are at the scene of the action. With all that is to be taking place in the emerging middle school, it is incomprehensible for decision-making powers to be completely centralized in the hands of the building principal. To require that all decisions regarding grouping students for instruction, curricular selections, as well as the use of time and facilities, be checked out with the principal for his approval would be to issue an invitation for the school to collapse. It would completely nullify one of the basic ingredients of the school, namely teacher freedom and responsibility.

Since the middle school is a highly complex structure operating on a nongraded basis, with teams of teachers making decisions about grouping and scheduling their students, it requires the employment of highly qualified specialists to help it achieve its stated objectives. To encourage staff to develop new curricular programs, to help teachers diagnose specific student needs, to initiate independent study programs, demands the presence, in the building, of trained personnel who have been given authority in the areas assigned to them. Only in this way can the group function as a leadership team.

The interdisciplinary and related arts teams, with the freedom afforded to them, can work cooperatively with the building leadership team, to create an organizational framework suited to the needs of today's early adolescents.

Chapter 3

Curriculums for the
Emerging Adolescent

THE MERE ESTABLISHMENT of a new organizational structure in a school has little positive effect on students and staff unless accompanied by alterations in instructional practices and in curriculum. Just as changes in the administrative structure of a school must be coupled with a change in certain instructional practices, departures from previously existing instructional procedures must, by the same token, be coupled with changes in the curriculum.

This chapter will concentrate on the types of curricula essential for the growth of early adolescents, and the goals that should be achieved by teachers and students. It will also present specific examples of curricular programs designed to achieve these expectations.

Curriculum Defined

Numerous books and pamphlets have been published that purport to contain all the material to be incorporated into the so-called English, Social Studies, Mathematics, Science, Home Economics, Industrial Arts, etc., curriculum for the early adolescent. The manuscripts generally contain lists of skills to be mastered and concepts to be explored, mentioning specific examples of approaches strongly recommended to achieve these goals. Depending on the influence of the individual state departments of education and the existence or the lack thereof of a statewide achievement level testing program in various disciplines, these lists either assume the form of guidelines or become a series of mandates. Whatever the case may be, in the minds of the public and in the minds of many people in the educational field, the term "curriculum" refers to a fixed body of knowledge that all individuals need to know. Such a concept has tended to destroy the curiosity and the initiative of thousands of students and their teachers over the decades.

It must be recalled that one of the basic purposes of the middle school is to help students become independent learners. This necessitates the establishment of an ungraded organizational structure. The nongraded pattern holds no respect for the idea that the curriculum consists of fixed subject matter assigned to definite age level groupings.

The curriculum must therefore be considered as that which the student is exposed to that is selected by the teacher and/or the student to enable the individual youngster to grow intellectually, emotionally, socially, and physically. The curriculum is open-ended and can consist of anything deemed appropriate in the professional judgment of the teacher. This points out one of the greatest problems faced by schools attempting to develop nongraded programs. Many schools are nongraded in name only because their instructional program is still predicated on the same curricular base as the graded school. The subject matter is laid out in a rigid, sequential fashion, minimal expectations are established for different age levels, and all students are expected to pursue the same program in a uniform fashion.

In the middle school, the emphasis must be on the learning process itself. The concepts to be understood, many of which will be universal in nature, and the skills to be mastered, which will often be multidisciplinary in scope, will be of primary curricular importance. The particular subject matter used to help the student comprehend these concepts and acquire these skills will be of less importance. Thus the emphasis shifts from learning definite answers to specific questions and acquiring lists of facts, to learning those processes by which answers to new problems as yet unencountered can be discovered.

Curricular Goals

Teachers in the middle school are expected to develop instructional programs appropriate for their students. Such programs should encompass definite skills and processes to be mastered over a span of several years. But in order to do this there must be a priority established that places the student and his specific needs first in the minds of his teachers, with the subject matter occupying a secondary position of importance. This is contrary to the traditional junior high school view of curriculum.

The curriculum of most junior high schools is subject matter oriented. The internal structure of the discipline itself is seen to determine how it should be organized and given to the student for consumption. The pupil is expected to learn all the material, which is usually presented in either chronological sequence or in varying degrees of abstraction. While today in most schools lip service is given to the importance of individualizing instruction, little is actually done to achieve this goal if all youngsters in a classroom, or in a grade, are given the same textbook, the same assignments, and the same tests and quizzes. For the sake of completing the curriculum this approach to instruction ignores the skills that must be mastered and the concepts that must be understood to achieve success in the future.

With youngsters in this age bracket undergoing so many physical and mental changes, there are vast differences among middle school students, and thus they have different curricular needs that must be met. Thus it is easy to comprehend why students of this age need to:

1. Acquire proficiency in specific skill areas;

2. Be exposed to concepts or ideas that go beyond rigid subject matter boundaries;

3. Have an opportunity to explore areas of the curriculum with which they are not familiar;

4. Begin to grasp the important processes that are interdisciplinary and universal in nature.

It should be noted that none of the previously mentioned objectives specifies a particular segment of a set curriculum, such as the life cycle of a paramecium or the French and Indian War, that must be covered by all students. The flexible middle school curriculum by its very nature allows each teacher in coordination with his colleagues on his teaching team, to exercise his professional judgment in the selection of those items that will be used by different students in helping them to increase their knowledge.

This is the only logical way to structure a flexible curriculum. The tremendous knowledge explosion that has occurred within the last ten years has made it impossible for any individual, student or teacher, to grasp all the facts. This is why man has invented information retrieval systems. These mechanical devices bring needed factual material to man's attention within seconds. Thus there is no longer a need to learn all this factual information, only a necessity for knowing the means whereby this knowledge can be obtained and more importantly how it can be used.

This means that the teacher must no longer be required to fill the pupils' heads with many so-called vital, but unrelated, facts, often no more than trivia, but he must help the student to comprehend the process of how to acquire knowledge, and thus help the pupil to become an independent learner. This leaves the choice of appropriate subject matter very flexible.

Students must be taught how to read, write, and speak correctly; how to add, subtract, multiply and divide; how to spell; and grasp all the other essential skills without which they will be unable to function effectively in later life. Some of these skills have been part of the basic educational system for years. But the students must be helped to acquire these basic, vital skills, along with the skills of logic and human understanding, in a context that has meaning and importance to them if they are to be motivated sufficiently to gain proficiency in them.

Teachers and administrators, as well as parents, have been continually stating that early adolescents have difficulty with the following important intellectual processes:

Identifying	Analyzing
Defining	Comparing
Organizing	Predicting
Observing	Classifying
Discriminating	Interpreting
Deducing	Evaluating
Inferring	Concluding
Recognizing	Summarizing

Applying

Adults have some of these same problems.

This author contends that the reason why these processes, and the skills inherent in them, have not been grasped is because the schools have not been organized in ways that permit curriculums to be developed that would enable these processes, and the skills associated with them, to be emphasized and hopefully mastered.

Recommended Course Offerings

Considering the age level of students to be housed in the middle school, there should be a mixture of required and elective courses of study. It is recommended that the required course offerings consist of English, Social Studies, Mathematics, Science, and Physical Education.

It is suggested that students be allowed to elect courses in the following areas:

1. French,
2. Spanish,
3. German,
4. Music,

  5. Art,
  6. Home Economics,
  7. Industrial Arts,
  8. Typing,
  9. Band,
 10, Orchestra,
 11. Chorus, and
 12. Any other courses deemed to be of interest to students and parents of a particular school community.

There will be those associated with these elective areas who will challenge the decision to make their area one of choice rather than a requirement. They will immediately question the reasons for mandating the study of English, Social Studies, Mathematics, Science, and Physical Education and not their own area. It must be realized however that in today's world these five courses are thought to possess the ingredients, the skills, concepts, and processes necessary for survival. Since these areas were the core of instruction in the elementary school, it is essential that the students' education be continued in these subjects in the middle school in order to reinforce skills learned, and expose students to new concepts that incorporate these skill areas. This is in no way meant to demean the elective subject matter areas. They too can and do make significant contributions to the education of early adolescents, particularly when they are selected as a matter of choice based on interest.

For years junior high school students have been traditionally required to take ten weeks of art, ten weeks of music, and twenty weeks of either Industrial Arts or Home Economics, depending on their sex. This was known as cycling. The student was forced to take these courses whether he liked them or not. His individual preferences were generally disregarded. Until recently girls seldom if ever took Industrial Arts. Boys were rarely found in Home Economics classes. But aside from this, little else has been done to make the related arts areas completely elective.

This author contends that a youngster of this age should be allowed to take elective courses and continue with them as long as he wishes. Part of the learning process of a student should be the experience of making some decisions that will directly affect his own education. The school must help the students become discriminating selectors from among the wide assortment of electives available to them. It should be emphasized that mere whim will not be sufficient to allow a student to elect or reject a course. The ultimate decision as to which electives a student will pursue will depend upon:

  1. The interests of the pupil;

2. The student's ability;
3. Parental considerations;
4. Teacher recommendations;
5. Recommendations of the guidance counselor; and
6. Availability of teaching personnel.

Related arts personnel will argue that youngsters of this age must be exposed to all of their areas if they are to make intelligent decisions about pursuing further studies in one of these disciplines. Such an argument presumes that middle school students have had no exposure to these areas. Considering the technological world in which they live, and particularly the impact of television and do-it-yourself projects, students today are more sophisticated in these areas than in previous years, and thus they have a better basis for making their selections. If a student has a strong interest in art for example, that youngster should be allowed to take art daily for all three years of his middle school experience if he so desires. Why must he be cycled out after ten weeks to go into another resource area in which he has no interest?

Cycling creates a fragmented approach to the related arts area. It prevents a student from pursuing an area of interest in depth, and thus never allows him to become truly proficient in the skills of the discipline. Such an approach to scheduling is not in keeping with the middle school's philosophy of individualized instruction.

An orientation program should be established that helps students and their parents learn more about the elective course offerings. Prior to the scheduling of elementary school students for their first year in the middle school, it is a good idea to hold an open-house in the evening at which time the building leadership team will explain the various program possibilities available. At the end of the briefing students and parents should be conducted on guided tours of the elective areas, introduced to the teachers, and be given brief descriptions of the course offerings by members of the staff. An opportunity could also be provided for elementary school youngsters and their parents to visit the middle school during the day to see these related arts areas in operation. This type of approach should give both parents and students a good basis for making appropriate selections from the list of electives available.

Figures 3-A and 3-B indicate two possible forms that can be used to ascertain student elective preferences. Figure 3-C illustrates the traditional form that has been used in many junior high schools and is being used in those middle schools that wish to program youngsters into elective areas on a cycle basis. Each form however is similar in that it requires the signatures of the parents, the pupil, and the guidance counselor prior to actually scheduling the student.

Student's Last Name _____ First Name _____ Date _____ Name of School _____

Area I. YES NO If "YES" circle order of preference.

	YES	NO					
Art	___	___	1st	2nd	3rd	4th	5th
Music	___	___	1st	2nd	3rd	4th	5th
Home Economics	___	___	1st	2nd	3rd	4th	5th
Industrial Arts	___	___	1st	2nd	3rd	4th	5th
Typing	___	___	1st	2nd	3rd	4th	5th

Area II. YES NO If "YES" circle order of preference.

	YES	NO			
Band	___	___	1st	2nd	3rd
Orchestra	___	___	1st	2nd	3rd
Chorus	___	___	1st	2nd	3rd

Area III. Please check one:

French _____ No language _____

Spanish _____ Either French, Spanish, or German _____

German _____

_____ _____ _____
Signature of Parents Pupil's Signature Guidance Counselor

Figure 3–A
Elective Choice Sheet

Dear Parents:

Your child will be entering his (first) (second) or (third) year in the middle school in September. His program of studies will include English, Mathematics, Science, Social Studies, and Physical Education. In addition, he will be given an opportunity to select (1) Industrial Arts, (2) Home Economics, (3) Art, or (4) Music. Band and Chorus are open to all students and may be elected by those who are interested.

For those students who have the capability, the motivation, and the maturity to begin or continue with the study of a foreign language, we are offering French, German, and Spanish.

In order to schedule your child for his courses in the Middle School next year, it will be necessary for us to know his choices in the above areas. Please fill out the form below, indicating your preferences and return to your child's homeroom teacher.

Student:_____ Date:_____

Present Grade:_____ Homeroom Teacher:_____

Check First and Second Choice:

_____FRENCH _____GERMAN _____SPANISH _____NO LANGUAGE

_____Continue _____Begin

CHORUS _____ YES _____NO IF YES, PLEASE INDICATE:

BAND _____ YES _____NO INSTRUMENT_____

EXPERIENCE_____

_____INDUSTRIAL ARTS _____ART

_____HOME ECONOMICS _____MUSIC

_____
PARENT SIGNATURE

Figure 3–B
Elective Choice Sheet

Dear Parent:

Your child will be entering his (first) (second) or (third) year in the Middle School in September. His program of studies will include English, Mathematics, Social Studies, Science, and Physical Education. In addition, he will be given an elective program of (1) Industrial Arts, (2) Home Economics, (3) Art, and (4) General Music. A change in the elective program will be made at the end of each twelve-week period. Band and Chorus are open to all students and may be elected by those who are interested. Both Band and Chorus are full year courses.

Those students who are already taking a foreign language will continue with the program. For those students who wish to begin the study of a foreign language, we are offering French, German, and Spanish.

In order to schedule your child for his courses in the Middle School next year, it will be necessary for us to know what his electives are. Please fill out the form below indicating your preferences and return to your child's homeroom teacher.

STUDENT:_____ DATE:_____

PRESENT GRADE:_____ HOMEROOM TEACHER:_____

PLEASE INDICATE YOUR CHOICES IN EACH AREA.

I. FOREIGN LANGUAGE   Check one:

_____Continue Present Language. _____Begin a Language.

Number first and second choices.

_____FRENCH _____GERMAN _____SPANISH _____NO LANGUAGE

II. MUSIC

CHORUS   ____YES ____NO   If yes, indicate:_____
BAND   ____YES ____NO   Instrument_____
                           Experience_____

III. Resources

Please make three choices for the entire year. Number your choices in order of preference. HOWEVER, KEEP IN MIND THAT IT MAY NOT BE POSSIBLE TO GIVE YOU YOUR CHOICES IN THE ORDER YOU HAVE INDICATED.

__Wood Shop __Metal Shop __Graphic Arts __Home Economics
__Art   __General Music

PARENT SIGNATURE

Figure 3–C

Cycling Approach to Elective Scheduling

It must be kept in mind that youngsters of this age are changing in many ways. They have interests in many areas, and the intensity of their interest is subject to rapid change. Taking this into account the school must allow programs to be developed and schedules to be created that will compensate for this condition.

Once signed up for a course or a series of elective courses, the student should be permitted to remain in that program until he expresses a definite desire to drop it for specific reasons. At that point the guidance counselor should:

1. Meet with the student and explore his reasons for dropping the course.

2. Discuss the matter with the teacher whose course the student wishes to discontinue.

3. Contact the parents and make them aware of the situation.

4. Give his professional recommendations to the parents, the student, and the teacher.

5. Inform the building principal and the instructional consultant prior to the final decision.

6. Have the parent sign a form indicating that their child has permission to drop the course.

7. Meet with the youngster again in an attempt to schedule him into other elective areas in which he may have an interest.

The purpose of this seven-step procedure is not to discourage the pupil from dropping a course, but to help him realize what he is doing and why. It also keeps the parents fully informed of the student's progress in school.

It should be understood that a student can be allowed to take as many electives as his schedule will permit. The youngster could, if he so desired, elect to take Music for ten weeks, Home Economics for twenty weeks, and Art for ten weeks. Thus students could develop their own cycle schedule through the elective areas, but in actual practice this type of program selection rarely occurs.

Experience has shown that establishing elective courses in the middle school also causes teachers to spruce up their programs, make them more interesting from a student's point of view, and engage in professional competition with colleagues in other elective areas. Middle schools that have been in operation for several years have determined that student enrollment does not decrease in resource areas where students and teachers are working together to create exciting instructional programs. If the student decides to select a resource area for study, he is usually willing to give it a fair trial. Since there are ordinarily more students wanting to take a particular course than there are teachers available to teach it, it creates, in a sense, waiting lines among the students for favorite courses at certain points in time. When a vacancy exists in the classroom of an elective area, a student is taken from the waiting list to fill that spot.

Since students know that once they drop a course there may not immediately be room for them in another desired elective area, they are a bit reluctant to drop a program unless guaranteed admission into another elective area. If they could not gain admission into the desired elective, they would either have to select another resource program, perhaps not the one of their choice, or else be scheduled into a study hall or student commons area.

Since student preferences are honored where possible, and since sound procedures have been established for dropping courses and enrolling in new ones, this plan creates a very stimulating environment for students and staff.

In conclusion, it should be pointed out that if students are to be given freedom of choice in the matter of electives, they must also be free to elect not to take any resource subjects. This may strike some educators as unsound. But if students are to be given a certain amount of responsibility, the school must give them an opportunity to exercise this prerogative by making an inappropriate decision in an area that won't severely handicap them in the future. The natural enthusiasm of middle school youth makes ninety-nine percent of them eager to pursue most electives.

A situation may arise however in which instruction in an elective area is poor, students drop the course, and other youngsters decide not to enroll in it. Although such instances should be the exception rather than the rule, in such a case as this, there is no longer a need for that course and for that teacher. If the teacher is not on tenure there is no problem. If he is on tenure but cannot teach any other subjects, the individual is let go until such time as there is a need once again for his professional services.

Interdisciplinary Unit #1—The Sea Around Us

In Ft. Lauderdale, Florida, during an intensive, month long in-service program for middle school personnel at which time students of middle school age were available on a volunteer basis to aid in the experimental program, a unit was developed which demonstrates how teachers and students can use events of national interest as motivation for practicing basic skills and comprehending new concepts. The United States had just launched Apollo 11 and the entire world was about to watch the first moon walk, the return trip to earth, and the splashdown. Considering the school's close proximity to Cape Kennedy and the natural geography of the environment, student and staff interest in the project was very high. It was mutually agreed upon by one interdisciplinary team and its students to study certain aspects of the sea and relate them, where possible, to the Apollo project.

The mathematics teacher and the social studies teacher on the team worked with students in helping them to trace routes leading to the splashdown area. After the students had indicated that they would like to travel to the target area on the Queen Elizabeth, a former passenger ship permanently based in the Ft. Lauderdale area, the math teacher gave them the information in Figure 3-D, in the form of a ditto sheet.

Your mission is to charter the Queen Elizabeth now located in Port Everglades, Florida. After chartering the Queen you must plot a course that will take you to an area in the Pacific Ocean where you will assist in recovering Apollo 11. The location of the splashdown area is 175 degrees east, 10 degrees north. Your goal, after considering the factors listed below in addition to other discoveries you make, is to get to the target area as quickly as possible. Give the course you will take, the total hours of the trip, and the time and date of your arrival.

You will have to consider the following:

    A. Latitude.
    B. Longitude.
    C. Time.
    D. Ocean Currents.
    E. Possible courses to the splashdown area.
    F. Ship capabilities.
    G. Length of the Queen Elizabeth—1083 feet.
    H. Draft—56 feet.
    I. Length of anchor chain—165 fathoms.
    J. Fueling range based on a twelve boiler operation:
        1. 30 kts. for 3500 miles.
        2. 15 kts. for 6000 miles.
        3. 25 kts. for 4500 miles.

Figure 3-D
The Sea Around Us—Mathematical Aspect

The social studies teacher worked with her pupils on map and globe skills and students plotted various courses for the trip. She secured a film entitled "The Restless Sea" which helped many youngsters comprehend the geographic factors that had to be considered in reaching their destination. Other films produced by Jacques Cousteau were also used to highlight points raised by the pupils in their investigations.

The English teacher on the team, with the cooperation of the librarian, had all the books in the library dealing with the sea moved into the classrooms where they were available for immediate student use. In her vocabulary development she focused on the following terms, all of which were directly related to the topic under discussion:

1. Bathysphere	15. Dredge
2. Plankton	16. Scuba
3. Oceanography	17. Trenches
4. Desalinization	18. Buoy
5. Algae	19. Modules
6. Mohole Project	20. Tide
7. Current	21. Edible
8. Undertow	22. Mariner
9. Continental Shelf	23. Prime Meridian
10. Thermocline	24. Drift
11. Hydrosphere	25. Knots
12. Sounding	26. Course
13. Fathom	27. Bends
14. Time	28. Triests

The science teacher on the team worked with the students in exploring some of their ideas about life in the sea, both plant and animal. The students were eager to touch and feel examples of plant and animal life found in the sea. Therefore some youngsters were taken by a teacher out on a boat to gather specimens. They caught fish and brought in several varieties of seaweed which would be used in the classroom by other students. For several days the pupils went about dissecting the fish, looking at the seaweed through a stereo viewer, see Figure 3-E, and viewing some filmloops about sea life. Students were also asked to find answers to the following questions:

1. What are fish?
2. How do fish take in oxygen?
3. What is their means of travel?
4. What is the purpose of fins?
5. How are fish able to rise in the water?

At this point the English teacher worked with some pupils on their written expression. He also aided pupils in keeping a log of their activities throughout the three-week period that this topic was being explored.

While one interdisciplinary team was focusing on this topic with its students, certain members of the related arts team joined in the undertaking. The art teacher had interested students painting sea scenes and decorating the classrooms of the interdisciplinary team with appropriate

One of your classmates has gathered some seaweed from the ocean. Please examine it carefully and look for any types of eggs or small animals which could or may be found in the seaweed. This can be done by placing a small sample in the petri dish and adding several drops of water. Either draw a picture of what you see or write a description of what you observe.

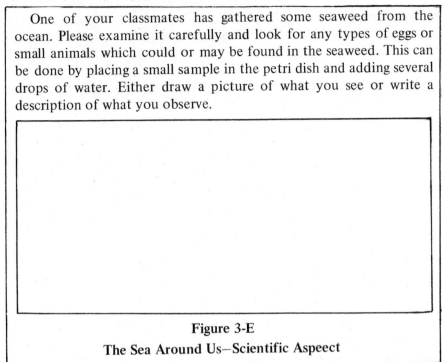

Figure 3-E
The Sea Around Us—Scientific Aspeect

materials designed to fit in with the sea theme. The physical education staff also worked with some students on the basic principles of surfing and body navigation through water. Two young high school graduates were invited in to speak with the students about:

1. Where they surf.
2. Why they surf.
3. Composition and structure of a surfboard.
4. Techniques of surfing.

The class was very receptive to their presentation and responded with many questions.

This interdisciplinary unit, developed in the course of a three-week summer session, through the cooperation of students and staff, was most successful. It developed certain fundamental skills while enabling the pupils to see that many of these skills applied to several subject matter areas simultaneously. It also helped staff to see that such an approach, based on student interests, can work in helping youngsters achieve worthwhile objectives.

Interdisciplinary Unit #2—The Airport

Topics of local interest can also be used as a basis for developing significant interdisciplinary units. Al Cappalli, principal of the Peconic Street Junior High School in Ronkonkoma, New York, and members of his staff capitalized on the tremendous interest generated by a proposal to build a jetport within their school district to create such a unit.

For some time there had been considerable discussion as to the location of a proposed fourth jetport in the New York metropolitan area. Kennedy, Newark, and La Guardia airports were not capable of handling all air traffic for the area. Since MacArthur Airport, in the town of Islip, was only 60 miles from New York City, it was natural that the sight would be considered as a possible fourth major airport. One interdisciplinary team and its students decided to study the impact that such a jetport would have on their community.

The members of the interdisciplinary team, Gail Griffith, English teacher; Jack Randazzo, Mathematics teacher; Al Ventura, Social Studies teacher; and Donald Daum, Science teacher, felt that the jetport topic was broad enough to encompass a sufficient number of skills and concepts related to their respective subject matter areas and thus appeal to a wide variety of student interests. The teachers also felt that this project would make learning come alive for their pupils by focusing on a relevant issue. If things worked out as planned, and they did, the students would have a clearer understanding of the many issues surrounding a proposal that could directly affect their lives, while realizing that learning could be enjoyable.

Students on the team visited the local airport and then all 125 of them traveled to Kennedy Airport to view the facilities and conduct interviews with residents in the area about how air traffic affected their lives. The students were particularly interested in the air and noise pollution created by the planes. This field trip received considerable coverage in the local press and earned the school, the team, and the students a good deal of praise.

Prior to launching the airport project it was decided that student progress would be evaluated in terms of the individual's ability to respond to the questions listed below as well as on their participation in various activities associated with the study.

1. What is progress? Do people have the right to try to halt it?
2. How does "progress" change the physical appearance of a community?
3. How do people change? How do social changes come about?
4. Is turning MacArthur airport into a major jetport progress? How will it affect Ronkonkoma and neighboring communities? What are the benefits? problems? liabilities?
5. What voice does the community have in this matter? What voice *should* the community have?

6. How is aviation effecting changes in our life today?
7. What effects will new industries in Ronkonkoma have on the health and welfare of the people?
8. How has the advent of the airplane changed our way of life?
9. How is an airport operated?
10. What are the purposes of airplanes?
11. What are the vocational possibilities of an airport?
12. It has been said that the airplane has made the world smaller. It has also been said that the airplane has made the world larger for each of us. Explain.
13. Would the world be better off today if the airplane had not been invented?
14. One of the results of the growth of aviation has been the creation of new job opportunities for men and women. Give examples.
15. What are the advantages of a career in aviation? How does one prepare for such a career?
16. When airplanes were first invented, it was thought.that private planes might become as common as automobiles. Why has this not happened?
17. What are some of the unsolved problems in aviation with regard to noise? health? safety?[1]

Examples of some of the skills taught and concepts explored in the course of this month long undertaking are as follows:

English:

1. Students wrote letters to local and state politicians to ascertain their views on the location of the fourth metropolitan jetport.

2. Letters were written to local businessmen to determine how they felt the proposed jetport would affect their business.

3. Pupils wrote letters to possible guest speakers, developed publicity releases about the programs, and sent thank you notes to appropriate parties.

4. Students learned how to introduce guest speakers to an audience and how to moderate panel discussions.

5. Library resources were used extensively to locate material dealing with aviation and with the local community.

6. All spelling words and vocabulary development lessons were directly related to the airport project.

7. Oral reports were given on famous aviators, their flights, and on the history of the town and its government.

8. Students learned how to conduct interviews.

---

1. Albert Cappalli to George W. Graham, November 12, 1969, *Airport Unit,* Connetquot Central School District No. 7, Bohemia, New York, pp. 6-7. This unit was developed by the following members of the Peconic Street School: Donald Daum, Science teacher; Gail Griffith, English teacher; Al Ventura, Social Studies teacher; John Randazzo, Mathematics teacher; Karen Baer, Art teacher; Anthony Izzo, Music teacher; and Maureen Norton, Home Economics teacher.

9. Pupils read poems dealing with aviation such as:

   a. Darius Green and His Flying Machine,

   b. Radar,

   c. To An Aviator, and

   d. The First Aviator.

10. Written reports were prepared on the findings of different student groups.

Social Studies:

1. Students studied the possible sociological effects of the new jetport on families living in the immediate area.

2. The psychological effects of noise on mind and body were explored.

3. The growth of industry and business in the area was analyzed.

4. Real estate values and tax rates were forecast.

5. The importance of community planning was discussed.

6. The effect of aviation possibly creating a one world concept was explored.

7. The possible home building boom resulting from airport expansion and its influence on schools was studied.

  8. Construction of a model airport was undertaken.

9. The possible connection between noise levels and mental processes was analyzed.

10. Debates on the pros and cons of the proposed jetport were held.

Science:

1. A definition of sound was developed.

2. Students learned how sounds are transmitted.

3. Velocity as related to the density of the medium was analyzed in lab experiments.

4. Sonic booms were discussed.

5. The intensity of sound was demonstrated.

6. Thresholds of hearing and thresholds of pain were explored.

7. The Doppler effect was studied.

8. Temperature inversions were discussed.

9. Students worked with oscilloscopes, hearing devices, tuning forks, and stop watches in laboratory situations.

10. Health and its relationship to our economy was studied in detail.

Mathematics:

Some of the areas explored were:

1. Velocity—distance formulas.

2. Real estate finances and tax problems.

3. Flight costs and accounting procedures.

4. Scale drawings.

5. Using fixed formulas to solve problems.

6. Speed-time problems involving trains, cars, and planes.

7. Making graphs and charts.

8. Reports on the economic advantages of the airline industry.

9. Defending economically the pros and cons of the proposed jetport.

10. Deciding, on a mathematical basis, between the purchase of two homes in the school district.[2]

During the development of this unit, three members of the related arts team—Karen Baer, art teacher; Anthony Izzo, music teacher; and Maureen Norton, home economics teacher—worked cooperatively with the interdisciplinary team in helping students to fully comprehend the topic.

In Home Economics classes girls studied grooming techniques and the job possibilities offered by careers in aviation. They learned how to become an airline stewardess. Pupils also studied how foods are prepared for the airlines. This led them into the fields of prepackaged foods and infrared cooking, as well as into the area of economics.

The Art teacher worked with students in helping them to prepare political cartoons on the jetport controversy. Some of the material developed here demonstrated that certain students could apply their artistic talents to political situations and convey a definite message.

Music students were shown the relationship between noise, sound, and music, by means of a tuning fork, an oscilloscope, and a piano. This tied in with similar concepts being developed by the science teacher. Some of the other topics explored by students with the music teacher were:

1. Music vs. noise.

2. Regular vibrations and irregular vibrations.

3. Pleasing (consonant) tones and displeasing (dissonant) tones.

4. Pitch, diameter, and tension in string instruments.

5. Standing waves and length in wind instruments.

6. Hi-fi frequency.

Other Interdisciplinary Units

While international, national, and local topics can be used as focal points for developing interdisciplinary units, there are other concepts that can be studied that likewise have a universal appeal and a universal applicability. Such topics as:

---

2. *Ibid.*, pp. 8-12.

1. With freedom comes responsibility,
2. Modern man and the Renaissance man,
3. Fact vs. opinion,
4. The inductive approach vs. the deductive approach, and
5. The art and science of war

were used to help students acquire basic skills, and were related to situations existing today. If teachers and teams are attuned to their students and to the conditions and feelings existing in the world, there is no limit to the number of interesting units that can be created.

Summary

If the middle school is to achieve one of its primary goals, i.e., helping students to become independent learners by means of an individualized approach to instruction, then its teachers must be given the freedom to develop appropriate curricular offerings. This will demand that teachers know their students as individuals prior to the undertaking of program development. As teachers get to know their students better, it will become apparent that pupils will have different needs. Different skills will have to be stressed with different students. Various concepts will be grasped by some and not understood by others. This will necessitate the creation of programs specifically designed to help the individual student make continuous progress. To create such programs will place great demands on the inventiveness of professional personnel. Teachers must not be hindered in their efforts to meet this challenge by grade-level curricular barriers. They must be free to select from a vast array of knowledge and human experience, regardless of its previous grade-level designation.

Once given the freedom essential to create exciting programs for students, the staff can help pupils acquire proficiency in many different skill, concept, and process areas.

While teachers must have freedom to create, pupils must also have freedom to either select or reject certain course offerings. This freedom of choice and the manner in which it is handled can be an excellent learning experience for the students, the staff, and the school. It is imperative that students of this age level be allowed to have a voice in making some decisions that have a direct bearing on their own educational program. Sound techniques can be incorporated into course selection procedures that can preserve order while at the same time allowing a considerable amount of freedom.

Chapter 4

Staff Deployment –
Transition to
Interdisciplinary Teaming

THE NEEDS OF today's students and society have made the self-contained classroom obsolete for early adolescents. The ever increasing behavioral and intellectual demands of diverse student populations require a more efficient type of organization. The concept of the teaching team, which allows for the pooling of teacher talents, is perhaps the only organizational structure capable of meeting this challenge.

To secure the benefits of both the complete departmentalized structure of most existing junior and senior high schools, and the basic, self-contained pattern at the elementary level, it was decided in Englewood, New Jersey, and Liverpool, New York, to explore an interdisciplinary approach to teaming and to classroom instruction. Discussions between administrative staff and teaching personnel led to the decision to form four-member teaching teams, composed of one English, one Social Studies, one Science, and one Mathematics teacher per team. Each team was given the opportunity to group its students, schedule them, and develop curricular programs deemed appropriate for various individuals and groups of individuals assigned to the team.

Safeguards were developed to insure team efficiency. A master schedule and facility utilization chart were established that permitted each team to make those decisions that would directly influence its overall operation. Time and space were provided for daily planning sessions, and new procedures for recruiting and hiring personnel were employed that directly involved teachers in the decision-making process. The need for a team leader was explored as well as the emerging concept of the teacher team—student team. All of these problems and decisions have been faced and resolved with varying degrees of success by middle school staffs.

The Composition of the Team

Ideally the middle school, whether graded or ungraded, should be staffed by individuals highly skilled in a specific discipline and philosophically disposed towards the child-centered approach to instruction. In most junior and senior high schools teachers tend to focus on the students in terms of the subject to be mastered rather than on the broader concepts and processes that transcend the various disciplines. As a result, students are exposed to a disjointed educational program which fragments their learning.

This departmentalized approach, which focuses on mastery of facts within a single subject matter area, combined with the rigidity of the secondary schools' master schedule replete with predetermined modules of time, has severely crimped attempts to make creative use of time and space available to students and staff. This has resulted in little being done to integrate learning experiences between disciplines for the benefit of students. A glance at a typical schedule (Figure 4-A) for a seventh grade student in a traditional junior high school clearly demonstrates the inflexibility of the total operation as the student is forced to move from room to room, floor to floor, and subject to subject every forty-two minutes.

At the junior high school level English, Social Studies, Mathematics, and Science teachers are generally operating as either self-contained units or within the confines of a subject matter team. In either case the teacher is generally not only unaware of how his or her students are doing in the other subject matter areas, but is almost totally ignorant of the curricula being explored by the students within the other disciplines.

Figure 4-B depicts the deployment of those teachers responsible for a significant portion of the instructional program of Charles Rogers as they are forced to function within a traditional lock-step master schedule. As the schedule indicates, it is impossible for these teachers to meet together on a regular basis, within the confines of this eight-period day, to discuss Charles Rogers as an individual personality, and as a student who needs a particular instructional program.

At the upper elementary level, with the ever increasing specialization of knowledge within each discipline, and the increasing maturity of today's sixth grade students, the future of the self-contained classroom organizational pattern is very much in doubt. It is not realistic to expect the so-called sixth grade teacher to be competent enough in the language arts, social studies, science, and mathematics to meet all the demands of her twenty-five or thirty students in these areas. On the other hand, placing ten- and eleven-year-old youngsters in a completely department-alized structure would only compound the problem already in existence at the secondary level. The solution to the dilemma of determining the appropriate organizational framework within which students and teachers can operate effectively must lie somewhere in between the two extremes of complete departmentalization and a totally self-contained classroom arrangement.

Rogers	Charles	211	7
Last Name	First Name	Homeroom	Grade

Period	Time	Subject	Teacher	Room
1.	8:30 - 9:12	Math. 7	Jordan	221
2.	9:15 - 9:57	Phys Ed[1] —Study[2]	Masi	
3.	10:00 - 10:42	Social Studies 7	Scott	105
4.	10:45 - 11:27	French I	Latour	210
5.	11:30 - 12:12	Lunch		
6.	12:15 - 12:57	Science 7	Vars	215
7.	1:00 - 1:42	Ind Arts[3] —Music[4] Art[5]	Welch — West Baer	137-129 219
8.	1:45 - 2:27	English 7	Sheldon	101

1—Meets 3 days a week—M,W,F

2—Meets Tues & Thurs in cafeteria

3—First twenty weeks

4—Third ten weeks

5—Fourth ten weeks

Figure 4—A
Traditional Junior High School Schedule

Period	Jordan	Scott	Vars	Sheldon	Latour	Welch	West	Baer
1	Math 7*	Duty	Science 7	Prep	French II	Ind Arts 7	Music 8	Prep
2	Math 7	Soc Study 7	Science 7	English 7	Prep	Ind Arts 8	Music 7	Art 7
3	Prep	Soc Study 7*	Science 7	English 7	French I	Prep	Duty	Art 8
4	Math 7	Prep	Duty	Lunch	French I*	Ind Arts 7	Music 8	Art 8
5	Lunch	Soc Study 7	Lunch	Duty	French I	Lunch	Lunch	Lunch
6	Math 7	Lunch	Science 7*	English 7	Lunch	Ind Arts 8	Prep	Art 7
7	Math 7	Soc Study 7	Prep	English 7	Duty	Ind Arts 7*	Music 7*	Art 7*
8	Duty	Soc Study 7	Science 7	English 7*	French II	Ind Arts 8	Chorus	Art 8

*Indicates the period when Charles Rogers is present in the class

Figure 4–B

Traditional Junior High School Master Schedule

The interdisciplinary team concept can solve this quandary by capitalizing on the benefits to be gained by having students exposed to teachers well versed in a particular subject matter area, while cultivating the relationships that have previously existed between many students and their teachers in the self-contained classroom. Since all students in grades six, seven, and eight are required to receive instruction in the areas of English, Social Studies, Mathematics and Science, it was decided to establish interdisciplinary teams in the middle schools in Englewood and Liverpool. Each team would consist of four teachers: one English teacher, one Social Studies teacher, one Mathematics teacher, and one Science teacher.

In Liverpool, the initial concept of the interdisciplinary teaming of staff was the result of frequent classroom visitations and discussions with individual teachers by both the building principal and the instructional consultant. Each witnessed great overlapping in curriculum content among the four respective disciplines and saw tremendous possibilities for establishing a more logical and cohesive learning environment for students, as well as a more professionally stimulating environment for staff.

Since districts initiating middle schools will more than likely have to staff them at least partially from present staff at both the elementary and junior high level, it cannot be emphasized too strongly that a child-centered approach without the necessary expertise will not be sufficient to meet the demands of the middle school student. Neither will subject matter expertise suffice without the philosophical commitment to the child-centered, appropriately individualized curriculum approach to instruction.

Formation of the Teams

Teams must be composed of individuals not only proficient in a particular discipline, but possessing similar educational philosophies. The members of a team must also be personally compatible if the operation is to have a chance of succeeding. This willingness to work together will ultimately determine the success or failure of each teaching team, and is far more important than artificially trying to balance the sex or teaching experience factor on each team as has been postulated by various theories.

The leadership team, and especially the building principal, must talk with each member of the staff, not only to ascertain the individual teacher's thoughts about teaming, but to become aware of whom each might wish to work with on a team. While the building principal must make it perfectly clear to all parties that he has the ultimate responsibility for establishing the best possible learning environment for the students, he can still assure his staff that their wishes will be met where possible. The following case study of the Liverpool Junior High School as it evolved into the Liverpool Middle School will illustrate the importance of following such procedures.

Case Study: Liverpool, New York

In July, 1965, a new principal and a new instructional consultant were appointed to the staff of the Liverpool Junior High School, Liverpool, New York. The school itself, from all the information that could be gathered from an analysis of staff personnel folders and previous master schedules, was very traditional in its operations. Comments elicited from the superintendent, central office personnel, and members of the community confirmed this. Since the Board of Education, upon the recommendation of the superintendent, had endorsed the concept of nongradedness at the elementary level, and was planning to open three ungraded middle schools in September of 1966, a new leadership team was brought on the scene to bring the school into step with the district's overall philosophy of education.

Funds were provided to run a workshop during the last week in August, 1965, so that staff would be prepared for any new organizational patterns to be employed. Prior to the week's orientation program, the principal and the instructional consultant carefully analyzed the data contained in the teacher's folders, and discussed their analyses with the third member of the leadership team, the pupil personnel consultant. The woman occupying this position had been associated with the building since it first opened in 1953. She had been a mathematics teacher, a guidance counselor, and a vice-principal before assuming her present position. With the exception of the newly appointed teachers, she knew the total staff, its strengths and its weaknesses.

With the basic educational goals of the district very clear in the minds of the leadership team, it was decided to employ a modified subject-matter teaming structure that would serve as an initial step towards creating a flexibly scheduled, nongraded middle school for the following school year. The leadership team studied the staffing pattern approved by the board, Figure 4-C, and sought to deploy staff where it was judged they would be most effective.

Knowing only the approximate numbers of students at each grade level:

A. 215 ninth grade pupils.

B. 320 eighth grade pupils, and

C. 315 seventh grade pupils,

and the previous assignments of the staff, a master schedule was devised prior to the workshop. Of necessity, teachers were assigned to teams

without ever really having met the other members in order to prepare
materials and student schedules prior to the August orientation program.

Position	Number	Experience		
		R*	NS**	NBT***
English	8	5	2	1
Social Studies	8	4	2	2
Mathematics	7	6	1	—
Science	6	2	2	2
Foreign Language	5	2	—	3
Home Economics	2	2	—	—
Industrial Arts	2	2	—	—
Reading	1	—	1	—
Art	1	1	—	—
Music	1	—	—	1
Physical Education	2	1	1	—
Librarian	1	1	—	—
Music Teacher	1	1	—	—
Guidance Counselor	1	—	1	—
Leadership Team	3	1	2	—
TOTAL	49	28	12	9

R*—returning to our junior high school for another year.

NS**—new to the staff, but with previous teaching experience in
other schools.

NBT***—a new, beginning teacher with no previous experience.

Figure 4–C[1]
1965-1966 Junior High School Staff

This traditional approach to staff deployment resulted in the teaming
pattern illustrated in Figure 4-D. It clearly shows that a definite attempt
was made to balance each team with both new and experienced personnel.

After the first three days of the August workshop it was evident that
there were problems within most of the teams. There were frequent clashes
between "traditionalists" and the "experimentalists." Each camp sought
to conquer the opposition. When there were significant differences in the

---

[1]Robert J. McCarthy *How to Organize and Operate an Ungraded Middle School* (Englewood Cliffs, New Jersey: Prentice-Hall, Inc., 1967), p. 18.

Levels	Team	Staff	Experience		
			R*	NS**	NBT***
9	English	2	1	1	—
	Social Studies	2	1	1	—
8	English	3	1	1	1
	Social Studies	3	2	1	—
7	English	3	3	—	—
	Social Studies	3	1	—	2
7–8–9	Science	6	2	2	2
7–8–9	Mathematics	7	6	1	—
7–8–9	French	2	2	—	—
	Spanish	2	—	—	2
	French-Spanish	1	—	—	1
	Total	34	19	7	8

R*–returning to our junior high school for another year.

NS**–new to the staff, but with previous teaching experience in other schools.

NBT***–a new, beginning teacher with no previous experience.

Figure 4–D[2]

1965-1966 Junior High School Teams

ages of the team members, for the most part each went his separate way. Cliques were immediately formed, or in some cases, reformed and gaps widened between individuals.

The dissatisfied tone set during the workshop continued throughout the year. Analyzing the situation, the leadership team drew the following conclusions:

1. The staff was not prepared for moving so rapidly into a teaming situation.
2. The leadership team was not sufficiently acquainted with the staff to set up a good teaming situation wherein teachers could be teamed who would work well together.
3. Teams should not be formed simply by placing new with experienced personnel to achieve a so-called "experience balance." The personalities and the philosophies of the individuals to be teamed

---

[2]McCarthy, *loc. cit.*

is a more important factor to be considered than previous teaching experience or the lack of it.

The one-week workshop did however provide an opportunity for staff to come to grips with the problems inherent in teaming, and to comprehend some of the benefits to be derived from such an arrangement. Realizing that the make-up of each team was far from ideal, the leadership team decided to stick with the teams as they were, and work within this newly established structure, rather than create additional confusion and upset by shifting personnel.

The Junior High School Master Schedule

The six teams that were established for the 1965-1966 school year were:

1. A 7th grade English-Social Studies team composed of six teachers.
2. An 8th grade English-Social Studies team with six teachers.
3. A 9th grade English-Social Studies team with four teachers.
4. A five member Foreign Language team.
5. A six member Science team, and
6. A seven member Mathematics team.

The remainder of the staff operated within the limitations of the master schedule—Figures 4-E, 4-F, 4-G, and 4-H. This procedure scheduled students into periods with teachers for specific instructional programs. Since English and Social Studies classes for each grade level were not only scheduled back-to-back, but at the same time across grade lines, the teachers on these teams were encouraged to depart from the traditional 42-minute instructional period and use the two-period block of time as they saw fit.

Since most of the Science and Mathematics teachers were for the most part all teaching the same grade level at the same time, there was the opportunity to move a student from one group and one teacher to another group and another teacher. This schedule could also allow some teachers within these disciplines to make use of large group instruction (60-150 students), small group, seminar type instruction (10-15 students), as well as traditional class size instructional grouping (25-30 students).

Each of the six teams previously mentioned was provided with a common planning room and a daily planning period at which time all members of a team were free to plan with each other. As one might expect, with the limitations of the master schedule, and with only one week to get to know the staff on a personal and performance basis, all plans did not develop as the leadership team had hoped. Besides the

Periods	Cuff	Murphy	Mazzocki	Koeller	Smith, P.	Zepecki
1	Duty	Duty	Duty	Duty	Duty	Duty
2	English — 7	English — 7	English — 7	Soc. Stu. — 7	Soc. Stu. — 7	Soc. Stu. — 7
3	English — 7	English — 7	English — 7	Soc. Stu. — 7	Soc. Stu. — 7	Soc. Stu. — 7
4	Duty	Duty	Duty	Duty	Duty	Duty
5	Lunch	Lunch	Lunch	Lunch	Lunch	Lunch
6	Prep.	Prep.	Prep.	Prep.	Prep.	Prep.
7	English — 7	English — 7	English — 7	Soc. Stu. — 7	Soc. Stu. — 7	Soc. Stu. — 7
8	English — 7	English — 7	English — 7	Soc. Stu. — 7	Soc. Stu. — 7	Soc. Stu. — 7

Periods	Novara	Smith, S.	Martinsen	Hagan	Kelly	McKendrick
1	Prep.	Prep.	Prep.	Prep.	Prep.	Prep.
2	English — 8	English — 8	English — 8	Soc. Stu. — 8	Soc. Stu. — 8	Soc. Stu. — 8
3	English — 8	English — 8	English — 8	Soc. Stu. — 8	Soc. Stu. — 8	Soc. Stu. — 8
4	Duty	Duty	Duty	Duty	Duty	Duty
5	Duty	Duty	Duty	Duty	Duty	Duty
6	Lunch	Lunch	Lunch	Lunch	Lunch	Lunch
7	English — 8	English — 8	English — 8	Soc. Stu. — 8	Soc. Stu. — 8	Soc. Stu. — 8
8	English — 8	English — 8	English — 8	Soc. Stu. — 8	Soc. Stu. — 8	Soc. Stu. — 8

Figure 4—E

Seventh and Eighth Grade English-Social Studies Team Schedules, 1965-1966

Periods	Aitken	Smith, M.	Deloria	Hemmer	Brochetti	House
1	Prep.	Prep.	Prep.	Prep.	Math. — 7	Duty
2	Eng. — 9	Eng. — 9	Soc. Stu. — 9	Soc. Stu. — 9	Math. — 7	Math. — 7
3	Eng. — 9	Eng. — 9	Soc. Stu. — 9	Soc. Stu. — 9	Math. — 8	Math. — 8
4	Duty	Duty	Duty	Duty	Lunch	Lunch
5	Lunch	Lunch	Lunch	Lunch	Duty	Math. — 9
6	Duty	Duty	Duty	Duty	Math. — 9	Math. — 9
7	Eng. — 9	Eng. — 9	Soc. Stu. — 9	Soc. Stu. — 9	Math. — 8	Math. — 8
8	Eng. — 9	Eng. — 9	Soc. Stu. — 9	Soc. Stu. — 9	Prep.	Prep.

Periods	Hennessey	Tiernan	Deloff	Beck	Srinivasen
1	Math. — 7	Math. — 7	Math. — 7	Math. — 7	Math. — 7
2	Math. — 7	Math. — 7	Math. — 7	Duty	Math. — 7
3	Math. — 8	Math. — 8	Duty	Math. — 8	Math. — 8
4	Duty	Lunch	Lunch	Lunch	Duty
5	Lunch	Math. — 9	Math. — 9	Math. — 9	Math. — 9
6	Math. — 9	Duty	Math. — 9	Math. — 9	Lunch
7	Math. — 8	Math. — 8	Duty	Math. — 8	Math. — 8
8	Prep.	Prep.	Prep.	Prep.	Prep.

Figure 4—F

Ninth Grade English-Social Studies Team & Math Team Schedules, 1965-1966

Periods	Nettles	Quinn	Swerske	Michaud	O'Neil	Dore
1	Sci. – 7	Sci. – 7	Sci. – 7	Sci. – 7	Sci. – 7	Sci. – 7
2	Sci. – 9	Duty	Sci. – 9	Duty	Duty	Duty
3	Sci. – 9	Lunch	Lunch	Lunch	Lunch	Lunch
4	Lunch	Sci. – 9	Sci. – 9	Sci. – 9	Sci. – 9	Sci. – 9
5	Sci. – 8	Sci. – 8	Sci. – 8	Sci. – 8	Sci. – 8	Sci. – 8
6	Sci. – 8	Sci. – 8	Sci. – 8	Sci. – 8	Sci. – 8	Sci. – 8
7	Prep.	Prep.	Prep.	Prep.	Prep.	Prep.
8	Sci. – 7	Sci. – 7	Sci. – 7	Sci. – 7	Sci. – 7	Sci. – 7

Periods	Henry	Leopold	Steiner	Maga	Houser
1	French – 9	French – 9	Spanish – 9	Spanish – 9	French – 7
2	Prep.	Prep.	Prep.	Prep.	Prep.
3	Lunch	Duty	Lunch	Lunch	Lunch
4	French – 8	Lunch	Spanish – 8	Spanish – 8	Spanish – 8
5	French – 7	French – 7	Spanish – 7	Spanish – 7	Spanish – 8
6	French – 7	French – 7	Spanish – 7	Spanish – 7	French – 8
7	French – 9	French – 9	Spanish – 9	Spanish – 9	Duty
8	Duty	French – 8	Spanish – 8	Spanish – 8	French – 7

Figure 4–G

Science and Foreign Language Team Schedules, 1965-1966

Periods	Desens	Kreffer	Wells	Schwarts	Schillowski	Lindermann
1	I.A. – 8	I.A. – 8	Home Ec. – 8	Home Ec. – 8	Art – 8	Music – 8
2	I.A. – 8	I.A. – 8	Home Ec. – 8	Home Ec. – 8	Art – 8	Music – 8
3	Lunch	Lunch	Lunch	Lunch	Art – 7	Prep.
4	I.A. – 7	I.A. – 7	Home Ec. – 7	Home Ec. – 7	Art – 7	Music – 7
5	I.A. – 9	I.A. – 9	Home Ec. – 9	Home Ec. – 9	Lunch	Lunch
6	I.A. – 7	I.A. – 7	Home Ec. – 7	Home Ec. – 7	Art – 9	Music – 7
7	Duty	Duty	Duty	Duty	Art – 9	Duty
8	Prep.	Prep.	Prep.	Prep.	Prep.	Chorus

Figure 4–H

Industrial Arts, Art, Music, and Home Economics Schedules, 1965-1966

paramount problem of personality conflicts within the teams, other problems that emerged during the course of the 1965-1966 school year included:

1. *Staff division.* Each team of teachers became something of a school unto itself. Having their own planning rooms, they made little use of the faculty lounge. As a result there was very little dialogue and exchange of information among teams.

2. *Subject matter emphasis* by the staff. Since the teams that had been organized were subject matter teams, and in some instances grade-level teams, the teachers were concentrating mainly on their own disciplines and were generally unaware of, and not particularly interested in, any of the material being studied by their students in the other subject matter areas.

3. *Innovation without evaluation.* There were some individuals on these teams who did attempt to depart from the traditional pattern that they had previously operated in, but for the most part these teachers failed to evaluate not only their rationale for the innovation, but the effects of the new approach. This was particularly true where some tried to use large group instruction every day for several weeks, with no other purpose in mind than to save teacher time. Large groups of 60 to 125 students were instructed in almost the same fashion as regular-size classroom groups of 25 or 30 youngsters. The teachers involved in this operation usually carried on a Socratic dialogue with seven or eight students seated in the front of the room while the remainder of the class served as silent observers. Other individual staff members attempted to launch massive independent study programs which resulted in little more than typical study hall, teacher-directed assignments.

4. *Failure to regroup students* if to do so meant that students would have to be placed with another teacher. The administratively created, inflexible master schedule was the prime cause of this condition, and the fixed schedules developed by the teams themselves, especially the English-Social Studies teams, compounded the problem. Once the team had established an initial mode of operation and a grouping pattern, it was extremely reluctant to depart from it. Although certain members of a team might wish to do so, there was generally stiff opposition from the other members of the team to such a proposal.

Even though it is quite possible that a significant portion of these problems could have been avoided by the building leadership team by not establishing the composition of the teams until the end of the week's workshop, or that some of these difficulties, once uncovered, could have been resolved by decisions rendered by the building principal, it was decided to let the staff live with and work out their own problems, with the entire leadership team playing an advisory rather than an authoritarian role. This decision, although a difficult one to make and live with at the time, ultimately led to the establishment of one of the key strengths of the middle school structure, namely teacher and team decision-making responsibility and accountability.

Progress Made

Although many problems were discovered in the Liverpool Junior High School during the 1965-1966 school year, significant accomplishments were made in the following areas:

1. The complacency of a number of experienced teachers was rattled by the thoughts and ideas expressed by the new additions to the staff. While some staff members simply reinforced their previous assumptions about the teaching-learning environment, other experienced personnel began to reexamine their philosophical and educational positions and in so doing either developed a sounder basis for adhering to their former method of operating, or found a sound basis for trying some new instructional approaches.
2. Teachers new to the profession were able to learn a number of "tricks of the trade," some good and some bad, from their more experienced colleagues. This built up teacher confidence and enabled many neophytes to avoid those frustrations that often face the beginning teacher during the first few weeks in September.
3. Once the teaching staff realized that the leadership team was firmly committed to improving the educational climate of the building for students and staff, and not merely its own professional advancement, individual teachers began to discuss the school's operational and educational philosophy with the principal and/or the instructional consultant.
4. Gradually, as a result of conferences with the leadership team and with members of other teams, a large majority of the staff began to realize that they were unaware of what was taking place in subject matter areas other than their own and within other teams. This opened the door for further exploration of the interdisciplinary team concept.
5. Attempts were made to depart from the traditional organizational

rigidity of the junior high school by using large group instruction and initiating independent study programs.

6. Some of the teams that had experienced the greatest internal problems both during the workshop and the first few months of school, resolved many of these conflicts within the team itself, with a minimum of direction from the building principal and the instructional consultant.

7. Teacher aides were used effectively to give teachers more time to plan and to work more closely with their students.

8. Some English and some Social Studies teachers were beginning to plan cooperatively and develop curricular offerings and instructional procedures appropriate for the students assigned to them. Some no longer viewed themselves as simply subject matter specialists, but as members of a team.

Transition to the Middle School and Interdisciplinary Teaming

Discussions held with each member of the teaching staff indicated that the following features of the junior high school would definitely have to be abandoned if the middle school were to achieve its goal:

1. An inflexible master schedule.
2. Teachers assigned to teams by the building principal with little or no staff involvement.
3. An established curriculum to be covered by all students of a certain grade level.
4. Students assigned to teachers by chance.

From January through June of 1966, a series of lengthy conferences were held between the building principal and each member of his staff, as well as between each teacher and the instructional consultant. The leadership team had to determine by means of a frank, open-ended, confidential dialogue, what each teacher's feelings were about interdisciplinary teaming, and with whom each might be willing to work in a teaming situation. The results of these meetings were very productive. Teachers, realizing that the current year's operation was less than a total success for reasons previously mentioned, expressed a desire to give this new interdisciplinary approach a try.

Some of the reasons underlying the staff's willingness to undertake this innovation rested in the approach employed by the leadership team. While not necessarily guaranteeing that each teacher would be teamed with the person or persons of his choice, each faculty member was guaranteed that under no circumstances would he be teamed with an individual unacceptable to him. This assurance, combined with the possibility of being both responsible and accountable for scheduling, grouping and evaluating their students, presented staff with the opportunity to make those decisions vital to the successful operation of the school.

With the transition from a 7-8-9 junior high school to a 6-7-8 middle school, many ninth grade teachers had to decide whether they wanted to transfer to the high school or stay in the present building and become part of the middle school. Some, knowing what demands would be made of middle school staff members, requested and received transfers to the high school. Others, who were not granted a transfer, sought employment in neighboring school districts. Some others, not on tenure, were not asked to return for the following year because they did not represent the type of teacher well suited to the middle school student.

The district's transfer policy directed that any teacher desiring to transfer to another building within the district had to make this intention known to the present building principal before being interviewed by the possible receiving principal. The transfer required the approval of both building principals and the superintendent. This policy, combined with the fact that some staff were leaving the district, and that there was a decrease in middle school enrollment from that of the junior high, meant that there were six vacancies on the interdisciplinary teams yet to be formed, plus four other positions to be filled. The positions open were:

Science	1
Mathematics	1
Social Studies	2
English	2
Guidance Counselor	1
Music	1
Reading	1
Industrial Arts	1

Recruiting and Hiring Procedures

When interviewing candidates for the new middle school, it was decided to hire only those candidates who appeared to be very flexible, creative individuals. If a vacancy existed on an interdisciplinary team, it was also determined that team members would play a major role in the screening process.

The leadership team did the initial screening of all applications and made contact with candidates for purposes of setting up an interview. On the day of the interview, the building principal and the instructional consultant met with the candidate for about fifteen minutes at which time they tried to obtain some general information about his or her background and previous teaching experience. Other questions generally pursued at this time included:

1. What were your favorite high school and college courses? Why?
2. What were your most distasteful high school and college courses? Why?
3. Who were your favorite high school and college teachers? Why?
4. Who were the high school and college teachers you disliked the most? Why?
5. What kind of school are you looking to work in? Why?
6. What are your feelings on marking, report cards, and honor rolls?
7. What do you expect from your building principal? Why?

At this point the first phase of the screening process was terminated. The candidate was then taken to the planning room of the team that had the vacancy and the team then initiated the second phase of the screening procedure. Neither the principal nor the instructional consultant attended this second session. The interview with the team lasted anywhere from fifteen minutes to over an hour, the shorter interviews generally indicating that the team was not very interested in the candidate. From subsequent discussions with the candidates after these lengthy dialogues with the team, and from comments made by some team members themselves, the candidate was thoroughly grilled by his peer group. Many candidates indicated that this, the team interview, was the roughest they had ever been through.

If the team thought highly of the candidate, and if the leadership team made a similar judgment, the position was offered to the applicant. If either party had strong reservations about the individual interviewed, that person was not offered a contract. If the principal liked the candidate, but the team did not, that person was not hired. If the team liked the candidate and the principal did not, the person was not hired. If the principal liked the candidate and the team had neutral feelings about the applicant, a discussion between the team and the principal ensued, with the principal having the final decision. The same situation prevailed if the team liked the applicant and the principal had neutral feelings about the individual.

Thus both the teaching team and the administrative team had to agree on the credentials and potential of the candidate before an offer of employment would be made. This was indicated to the prospective middle school teacher during the course of the interviews and, if and when a teaching position was offered to the candidate, he or she knew that it in essence was a twofold endorsement of their expressed philosophy and practices.

The entire screening and interviewing operation was quickly eliminating from primary consideration candidates who were solely subject-matter oriented. Since the basic purpose for forming interdisciplinary teams was to establish teaching units that would focus on each pupil as a unique individual, both teachers and administrators quickly realized that it would be necessary to secure the services of individuals who would develop programs that their students needed, rather than resorting to the time-honored practice of forcing students to conform to predetermined curricular patterns.

In addition to this, various team members accompanied administrators on recruiting trips. This proved to be very successful especially when the teachers returned to the college or university from which they had recently graduated. The teachers usually had some good contacts in the new senior class and in the placement office. The teachers' enthusiasm for the new organizational structure was clearly demonstrated to those being interviewed and helped recruit new teachers.

As a result of these new recruiting and hiring procedures and the lengthy dialogues with returning staff members, the leadership team had sufficient information at its disposal to ultimately decide on the composition of each team. The final decision for teacher placement and team composition however had to rest with the building principal as he was the individual charged with the responsibility of seeing to it that the students assigned to each team received a good education.

After examining almost every possible combination of teaming situation, and keeping in mind such factors as desire to work with certain other individuals, personality traits, and philosophy of education, as well as the willingness to explore the curriculum of the other three disciplines, a consensus was reached between the leadership team and the teaching teams regarding the individuals to be placed on each team. Figure 4-I depicts the actual team assignments.

Block Time Scheduling

Once all vacancies had been filled and the make-up of each inter disciplinary team was determined, it was incumbent upon the leadership team to develop an organizational structure that would allow each team to function most effectively. Rather than simply substituting modular scheduling for the fixed period schedule previously in existence, it was decided to go a step beyond the modular schedule approach and give each team a large block of unscheduled time to work with their students. Using the standard forty-five minute classroom period as a guideline, it was decided to give each team four consecutive periods, thus giving them three continuous hours with their students for instruction in the areas of

| | | Years of | Traditional | Quiet[2] |
Teams	Sex	Experience	or Experimental	or Outspoken
TEAM M				
English	M	2	Experimental	Outspoken
Social Studies	M	4	Experimental	Outspoken
Mathematics[1]	F	10	Experimental	Outspoken
Science	F	2	Experimental	Outspoken
TEAM I				
English[1]	F	4	Experimental	Outspoken
Social Studies	F	1	Experimental	Outspoken
Mathematics	F	1	Experimental	Outspoken
Science	M	3	Traditional	Quiet
TEAM D				
English	M	1	Experimental	Outspoken
Social Studies[1]	M	13	Experimental	Outspoken
Mathematics	M	2	Traditional	Quiet
Science	F	6	Experimental	Outspoken
TEAM L				
English	M	13	Traditional	Quiet
Social Studies	M	1	Traditional	Quiet
Mathematics[1]	M	6	Experimental	Outspoken
Science	M	6	Traditional	Quiet
TEAM J				
English	F	1	Traditional	Quiet
Social Studies	F	3	Traditional	Quiet
Mathematics[1]	M	13	Traditional	Quiet
Science	M	1	Experimental	Outspoken
TEAM H				
English-Science	F	1	Experimental	Quiet
Mathematics-Science	M	13	Traditional	Quiet
Social Studies-Science[1]	M	13	Traditional	Quiet

[1] team leader [2] in dealing with students, teachers, and the Leadership Team

Figure 4–I[3]

Composition of Interdisciplinary Teams
1966-1967 Liverpool, New York

[3] *Ibid.*, p. 30.

English, Social Studies, Mathematics, and Science. Figure 4-J indicates how the teams were deployed within the block-time master schedule.

Within that three-hour block of time each team was given the freedom to operate as it wished and was encouraged to establish as many instructional groups within each discipline as was necessary for good instruction. Teams were told that it was not necessary, from an administrative point of view, for each teacher to meet with each instructional group every day. Teams actually operated as separate schools. What each team wanted to do with its students within that three-hour span would not affect the schedules of any of the other teams.

To further illustrate the responsibility given to each team of teachers, and the judgments they made, Figures 4-K and 4-L indicate how one team, in this case Team M, grouped its students for instructional purposes and made judgments regarding the amount of time needed by the different groups in each of the four disciplines over a two-day period of time. It should be noted that the team formed five instructional groups at this time. Since there were only four teachers on the team and only four rooms were assigned for their use, it was necessary not only to create a shifting, flexible schedule since there were more instructional groups than teachers on the team, but to allow the fifth group, not scheduled for instruction at a certain period of time during the three-hour block, to go to the library, student commons, or one of the learning centers.

In order to add greater variety to the program and to give teachers and students a different view of each other, it was also decided to flip-flop the entire master schedule every ten weeks. Thus, referring to Figure 4-J, teams M, I, and D met with their students within the 8:45-11:45 time block for the first and third ten-week segments of the school year. For the second and fourth ten-week segments, teams M, I, and D met with their students between the hours of 11:45 and 2:45. The other teams also switched their time blocks every ten weeks.

Teachers and students quickly observed differences with each other when meeting at different times of the day. Teams that initially met with their students in the 11:45-2:45 time block during the first ten weeks of the school year noticed that their students were far more alert, responsive, and achieved better test results when shifted into the 8:45-11:45 time block. Teams originally scheduled to meet with their students in the morning block of time noticed a slight decrease in student achievement when they met with their students in the afternoon. The greater gain in one group and the slight decrease in the other group was however in large measure influenced by the students assigned to each team and the personalities of the teachers assigned to each team. This is further explored in chapter 5.

Time	Team L	Team J	Team H	Team M	Team I	Team D
8:45 – 9:27	Planning Period	Student Commons and Learning Centers	Planning Period			
9:30 – 10:12	Learning Centers	Planning Period	Student Commons	English, Social Studies, Math and Science are taught in this block of time	English, Social Studies, Math and Science are taught in this block of time	English, Social Studies, Math and Science are taught in this block of time
10:15 – 10:57	Lunch	Cafeteria Duty and Planning	Learning Centers			
11:00 – 11:42	Cafeteria Duty and Planning	Lunch	Lunch			
11:45 – 12:27	English, Social Studies, Math and Science are taught in this block of time	English, Social Studies Math and Science are taught in this block of time	English, Social Studies Math and Science are taught in this block of time	Cafeteria Duty–Student Commons	Lunch	Lunch
12:30 – 1:12				Lunch	Learning Centers–Student commons	Cafeteria Duty
1:15 – 2:00				Learning Centers	Planning Period	Planning Period
2:05 – 2:50				Planning Period	Learning Centers	Student Commons

Figure 4–J

Block-Time Master Schedule for the Interdisciplinary Teams

8:45	English	Social Studies	Mathematics	Science
9:00		II	III	
9:15	I			IV
9:30		III	II	
9:45				
10:00	V	I	IV	III
10:15				
10:30				
10:45	IV	V		II
11:00			I	
11:15	III			
11:30		IV		V
11:45				

Each Roman numeral represents an instructional group.

Figure 4–K
Team M Block-Time Schedule–First Day

	English	Social Studies	Mathematics	Science
8:45				
9:00				
9:15				
9:30	II	V	IV	I
9:45				
10:00	I	III	V	IV
10:15				
10:30	III	II	I	V
10:45				
11:00				
11:15				
11:30	IV	I	III	II
11:45				

Each Roman numeral represents an instructional group.

Figure 4—L

Team M Block-Time Schedule—Second Day

This flip-flop in the master schedule every ten weeks also affected all other teachers. The foreign language, home economics, industrial arts, music, art, and physical education teachers noted distinct behavioral changes when they saw students at one time of the day as opposed to another. It was also noted that grades seemed to change for certain students as they were moved from one block of time to another.

An analysis of the flip-flop operation seemed to indicate the following:

1. Students react differently to the same teachers at different times of the day.
2. A student's achievement in a subject may be affected by the time at which he is scheduled for that subject.
3. Those less academically talented than others, that is, the average and below average students, seem to do better when scheduled for their academic subjects (English, Social Studies, Mathematics, and Science) in the morning and their physical performance subjects (Industrial Arts, Home Economics, Art, Music, Physical Education, and ALM foreign language) in the afternoon. It seems to fit both their alertness curve and learning styles.
4. The average and below average students experience fewer discipline problems when they meet with their interdisciplinary team in the morning and their resource area subjects in the afternoon than when the schedule is reversed.
5. The achievement of the above average and the excellent student is not significantly altered by meeting with the interdisciplinary team in the afternoon rather than in the morning. If there is any change, it only represents a slight decrease in the overall achievement, probably due mainly to both student and teacher fatigue factors.

In view of the above observations, while the flip-flop master schedule is an excellent technique for bringing flexibility to a school and of presenting both teachers and students with a different time dimensional view of each other, it has certain disadvantages. It is suggested that in the long run it might be more advantageous to the school as a whole, and especially to the average and below average students, if the interdisciplinary teams that they were assigned to meet in the morning time block rather than the afternoon one.

Modified Block-Time Schedules

The larger the block of consecutive time accorded to any team for instructional purposes, the more possibilities there are for more flexible and creative use of different modules of time within that time span. The shorter the duration of consecutive modules or periods of time assigned to the team, the greater the limitations placed upon the team and its decision-making prerogatives regarding the use of its time with its students. An examination of possible alternatives to the three-hour block of time is shown in Plans I, II, and III in Figure 4-M.

	Plan I	Plan II	Plan III
8:45			
9:00			
9:15			Interdisciplinary Teaming
9:30	Interdisciplinary Teaming		
9:45		Interdisciplinary Teaming	Resource Subjects
10:00			
10:15	Resource Subjects		
10:30		Resource Subjects	Interdisciplinary Teaming
10:45			
11:00	Resource Subjects		
11:15			
11:30		Resource Subjects	Resource Subjects
11:45	Interdisciplinary Teaming		
12:00		Resource Subjects	
12:15			Lunch
12:30			
12:45	Lunch		
1:00		Lunch	Interdisciplinary Teaming
1:15			
1:30	Interdisciplinary Teaming		
1:45		Interdisciplinary Teaming	Resource Subjects
2:00			
2:15			
2:30	Resource Subjects		Interdisciplinary Teaming
2:45			

Figure 4—M

Block-Time Scheduling Alternatives

In alternate Plan I, the team has three distinct, separate one-hour blocks of time at three different times of the day. This break-up of the three hours into three separate segments places limitations on the teaching team as it cannot plan on engaging in activities that last beyond sixty minutes because their students must then move to a resource area subject such as industrial arts, home economics, music, art, or physical education. While their students are scheduled into one of these resource periods, the team has its planning period. This type of modified block scheduling is employed in a number of middle schools that want to go beyond the traditional 45-minute period because they feel it is too short for instructional and activity purposes. The 60-minute instructional period, while slightly longer than the previous time module, still affords teachers little room for maneuvering time to suit their needs and those of their students.

Plan II shows teams being given 90 minutes of consecutive instructional time with their students at two different times during the day. This is really nothing more than a so-called double period, or a type of back-to-back scheduling. More frequently than not, classes and groups shift at the end of the first 45-minute period of time. This plan does however offer more possibilities for better use of time than the first plan.

Plan III is nothing more than a traditional junior high school schedule that allows each team to meet with its students for 45-minute periods at four different times during the day. Unfortunately this approach is passing for flexible scheduling within many middle schools solely because it allows the team to do what it wishes with its students during each 45-minute segment. Many middle schools still have the building principal, his assistant, or guidance counselors setting up the schedule and the grouping of students for each of these four periods, which are today often referred to as two consecutive 22-minute modules. The latter situation is a poor attempt to disguise an old, unimaginative schedule in new educational phraseology in order to impress the public and to give the teaching staff the feeling that their school is moving ahead under progressive educational leadership.

Insuring Team Efficiency

Since each team was given the responsibility for developing its own time schedule for meeting with its students within its three-hour time block, a procedure had to be established for informing students of their constantly shifting schedules if confusion was to be avoided. The four teachers assigned to each interdisciplinary team assumed the homeroom duties for all students placed on their team. The students were divided into four groups, at random, and placed in homerooms supervised by their teachers. Each morning the members of the team were able to inform their pupils, both verbally and in writing, what their day's schedule would be. Questions were answered, points clarified, and each pupil received a ditto copy of his schedule for that day, indicating where and at what time each of his different instructional groups would be meeting. These schedules were typed and run off by the teacher aide assigned to the team.

Each team was expected not only to develop daily, flexible time schedules, but was also asked to continually group and regroup its students in the areas of English, Social Studies, Mathematics, and Science. To accomplish these tasks a planning room was needed by each team. It was also imperative that all members of a team be free from all duties and responsibilities at the same time in order to plan together and work as a team. The block-time master schedule previously shown in Figure 4-J shows how time can be set aside for this purpose.

Small rooms in various areas of the building can be used for team planning rooms. A normal size classroom, between 760 and 840 sq. ft., can also serve as a planning room for two or possibly three teams. Since several teams are teaching while other teams are planning, eating, or holding conferences in resource centers with students, two or three teams operating on different time schedules can occupy the same room for planning purposes without interfering with each other.

All planning rooms were equipped with a desk, a chair, and a file cabinet for each member of the team. The teachers were also free to arrange and decorate the room as they wished. Some teams even brought in soft lounge chairs, a sofa, record players, coffee pots, and hot plates.

The Dilemma of the Team Leader Concept

Schools that choose to launch any type of teaming operation must ultimately decide whether or not to have team leaders. Some middle schools that have established either interdisciplinary teams or subject matter teams have felt that such a position was necessary to insure team efficiency. Generally, individuals are selected for such positions on the basis of their previous background and experience, plus a willingness to assume such a position. In most instances such selections are made by the building principal without staff involvement. Such authoritarian action is the antithesis of the cooperative spirit that is essential for the success of the middle school. If there is to be a team leader for each team, that individual must be selected, and approved of, by his teammates. If not, damaging results will occur.

In general, the duties and responsibilities that are incumbent on team leaders in an interdisciplinary arrangement are as follows:

1. To lead the entire team in a continual, thorough analysis and evaluation of each student's progress.
2. To plan and coordinate the constantly shifting schedules of all students and teachers composing the team.

3. Meet on a formal basis once each month with the leadership team of the building to discuss the team's operation.

4. To assume responsibility for the development and implementation of differentiated reading programs and diagnostic testing programs.

5. To continually strive to maintain a constant dialogue among all members of the team that focuses on each individual student as well as on logical attempts to coordinate material from the four disciplines.

To ask any individual to accept such a position without adequate financial remuneration would not be in the best interests of an industry striving for professionalism.

While team leaders can be an asset to middle school teaming, particularly when the program is being launched, in creating such a hierarchical position within the team framework, certain sacrifices are made. It must be understood that such a position tends to cause members of a team to look to the team leader for the solutions to many of their problems. Rather than attacking a specific problem as a four-member force, the team usually expects the team leader to resolve the matter, especially since he is receiving extra pay for the position. Thus with this type of arrangement, the only thing that has really been accomplished is the creation of another semi-administrative post in the organizational pattern of the building. The actual team spirit of mutual cooperation and concerted efforts by all members of the team has not been established, but rather thwarted.

Therefore if a middle school really wishes to initiate and perpetuate the team concept, the leadership of the team must come not only from within the team, but from various members at different times. An atmosphere must be created which allows for the realization of the concept of emerging leadership whereby different members of the team will assume, on an informal basis, leadership of the team depending on the time, situation, and circumstances. In this way a total team operation can exist and flourish.

Summary

Based on the premise that the subject matter specialist operating in a teaming arrangement with colleagues from other disciplines can best meet the needs of today's middle school students, an interdisciplinary approach was conceived. Analyses of both student and teacher schedules in existing junior high schools indicates that significant operational procedures must be changed if the middle school is to achieve its goals.

The teaching staff must be given greater decision-making prerogatives in the areas of curriculum development, grouping for instruction, use of time and physical facilities, and in recruitment procedures. A thorough examination of the steps undertaken by the Liverpool Junior High School, Liverpool, New York, as it shifted to a middle school organizational pattern, illustrates many of the phases that must be watched carefully throughout the transition. The errors made, the problems encountered, and the gains achieved in Liverpool can serve as a guide to schools in similar positions.

A simple master schedule based on the block-time concept, along with several examples of how teams have made creative use of the time allocated to them, demonstrates the operational climate that is essential to the success of an ungraded middle school.

The creative possibilities offered to the teaching and administrative staffs by an interdisciplinary teaming structure operating within an unstructured block of time are limitless.

Chapter 5

The Instructional Consultant

M OST TEXTBOOKS IN the educational field designate the building principal as the educational leader of the school. This is true. The staff that he assembles, the schedules that he develops, and the decisions he makes to a large extent determine what will take place within the school. But with the increased demands being made of administrators, the building principal can no longer be all things to all people. To be effective he must gather an administrative team that can function as a well organized unit to help students and staff achieve success. The various members of that building leadership team must be given great responsibility in the areas specifically assigned to each of them. Responsibility for appropriate curriculum development, as well as for instructional proficiency, should reside with the Instructional Consultant, a vital member of the building leadership team.

This chapter will explore the role of the Instructional Consultant in the middle school, the need for the position, and how it fits in with the leadership team concept. In addition to this, the relationship of the I. C. to the teachers, the teams, the building principal, and central office personnel will be analyzed. A typical two-day working schedule for the consultant will be described along with other demands made upon the office. A thorough understanding of the rationale behind the position and the workings of it is one of the keys to comprehending the operations of a successful middle school.

The Role Defined

The individual appointed as the Instructional Consultant should be a generalist with regards to his academic background and, at the same time, a specialist in working closely with people. He must be able to create environments within which people can do their best. While the I. C. is concerned with curriculum and instruction, he is primarily dealing with human beings. He must realize that if he expects curriculums to be analyzed, modified, or changed, or if he wants instructional practices to be altered, he must bring about change in the teachers themselves. In reality teachers are the curriculum and the instructional practices. To alter either or both of these requires that the professional change. This is the task of the I. C.

Therefore the Instructional Consultant should

assist teachers in the examination of their present beliefs and of the values they hold, and assist them in modifying those beliefs and values in light of the changing needs of children and society and the findings of research in child growth, development, motivation, and learning.[1]

This is his key function. He must cause teachers to look in and at themselves and what they are doing, and relate to the needs of the student populations they serve.

The Instructional Consultant should serve as an advisor to the entire professional staff. He must stimulate some to action. He must work closely with others who desire to innovate. He must educate those who are opposed to change. He must serve as a counselor of teachers and a supervisor of the entire instructional program.

It is essential that the I. C. establish rapport with all members of the professional staff. Only then will teachers begin to confide in and share with him their problems, perceptions, and ideas. In his supervisory capacity the Instructional Consultant must help each teacher to assess not only appropriateness of his goals for the students, but also the effectiveness of his instructional procedures.

This dual role of supervisor and counselor is a very demanding one. It requires the I. C. to walk a delicate educational tightrope between the two related, but distinct fields. To do this the Instructional Consultant must:

1. Be an individual above reproach who adheres to the highest ethical and professional standards.

2. Have a sound educational philosophy that corresponds to that of the school.

---

1. Ross L. Neagley and N. Dean Evans, *Handbook for Effective Supervision of Instruction* (Englewood Cliffs, New Jersey: Prentice-Hall, Inc., 1964), p. 115.

3. Firmly believe that the educational process is of vital importance to the survival of mankind. He must be committed.

4. Express his thoughts and ideas in a manner easily understood by the various individuals and groups with whom he comes in contact.

5. Encourage staff to experiment, to try new ideas, and make learning an exciting experience for their students and themselves.

6. Possess the ability to view the classroom environment through the eyes of the teacher and through the eyes of the students.

7. Read widely to keep on top of the latest curriculum developments, instructional practices, and evaluative techniques employed in all subject matter areas.

8. Be idealistic while at the same time practical in his hopes and expectations for the school.

9. Work very closely with the other members of the building leadership team.

The Need for an I. C.

To fulfill the duties and responsibilities of the position itself, the Instructional Consultant must continually educate and re-educate staff. Too often in the past changes in curricular programs, instructional practices, or organizational patterns have been unsuccessful because of the failure to provide teachers with the education that would enable them to operate in a manner consistent with the innovation. Many ungraded programs have proven to be ineffective precisely because the teachers involved lacked sufficient knowledge of how to individualize their instruction or group and evaluate their students within the new framework.

The necessary re-education required by any significant change in the total operations of the school cannot be provided through infrequent classroom visitations by a building principal. In-service courses that meet after school also cannot meet this demand. The staff needs intensive and continuous education over a long period of time. This can only be done by an individual whose sole responsibility is instruction and curriculum. This is why the nongraded middle school needs to have an I. C. if it is to be successful.

Since the building principal must be concerned with many administrative tasks, and the pupil personnel consultant is basically involved with the guidance program, the I. C. is the only member of the leadership team available on a full-time basis to work in the areas of curriculum and instruction. It must be remembered that the success or failure of the ungraded middle school concepts hinges not only on its organizational framework and operational procedures, but on the teachers' belief that it provides an excellent opportunity to improve upon previously existing conditions. The Instructional Consultant must therefore devote his time and energies to the concerns expressed by staff. It would not be fair to expect teachers to attempt to make a new program work unless they were firmly convinced that the old program had serious deficiencies and its replacement was substantially better than the original.

This means that the I. C. must cause teachers to evaluate what they have been doing professionally and what they would like to be accomplishing. One of the best methods to accomplish this is to familiarize the entire staff, teachers, administrators, and counselors with what other school districts are doing in similar attempts to make learning exciting for early adolescents. It is strongly recommended that the following studies, all doctoral dissertations, be read in their entirety by the Instructional Consultant, and shared with the staff:

1. *The Relationship of the Teacher's Knowledge of the Student's Background to the Effectiveness of Teaching* by Horace W. Sturgis. This is a study of the extent to which the effectiveness of teaching is related to the teacher's knowledge of the student's personal background.

2. *The Use of Unusual Time Modules for Scheduling Secondary School Students* by Grant Ellsworth Thayer.

3. *Critical Requirements of Independent Study Based Upon an Analysis of Critical Incidents as Observed and Reported by Students and Instructors* by John Joseph Margarones.

4. *A Study to Determine Whether the Multiple Period Approach or the Single Departmental Concept Allows the Teacher Greater Opportunity to Gain Information About the Individual Student* by Samuel Robert Bennett.

5. *Relationship of Students' Estimates of Teacher Concern to Teaching Effectiveness* by Elizabeth Madeline Ray.

6. *An Analysis of Achievement Outcomes: Team Teaching and Traditional Classes* by Scott Dayton Thomson.

7. *The Philosophical and Psychological Foundations of the Core Curriculum in Educational Theory: 1918-1958,* by Rucker Sterling Hennis, Jr.

8. *Nongraded Middle School—Supporting Theory and Conceptualized Functional Model* by Donald Henry Eichhorn.

9. *The Middle School in Oregon and Washington 1965-1966* by Alvin Wendell Howard.

10. *Differences in Mental and Educational Development from Grades Six Through Nine and Implications for Junior High School Organization* by Stanley Gordon Sanders.

11. *A Study to Determine the Relationship Between the Position of*

Teachers on the California F. Scale and Their Disposition Toward Teamwork by Joseph Francis Perez.

12. *The Effect of Varied Subject Period Scheduling on Achievement in the Seventh Grade* by Walter Alexander Kearney.

13. *An Investigation of the Effects of a Seventh and Eighth Grade Core Program on Pupil Progress in Selected Areas in Senior High School* by Bernard Schwartz.

These dissertations can serve as a basis for further study and can help to direct the pattern of future research to be undertaken, such as visits to other districts, before programs are finalized.

In addition to this the Instructional Consultant should gather information pertaining to the areas of:

1. Diagnosis of student needs,
2. Instructional objectives,
3. Instructional strategies,
4. Individualized instruction,
5. Independent study,
6. Flexible grouping,
7. Frequency of class meetings,
8. Length of class sessions,
9. Continuous progress,
10. The relationship of the middle school to the elementary school and the high school,
11. The library as a learning center,
12. Student evaluation,
13. Creative use of facilities, and
14. Teaming, problems and benefits, from a wide range of sources, and be prepared to share them with interested parties.

To do this it is essential that the I. C. read widely in areas of current interest in all fields of intellectual endeavor, such as political science, the humanities, and race relations. In the field of education it is imperative that he read different subject matter journals and periodicals, and also be familiar with publications of the Association for Supervision and Curriculum Development (ASCD), as well as with books pertaining to the middle school movement. He must also be free to attend conferences on the middle school and on curriculum development.

Relationship of the I. C. to the Leadership Team

While the building principal most definitely sets the tone for the school and is the educational leader of the building, for better or for worse, the Instructional Consultant is the key position in the middle school organizational pattern. It is the I. C. who, not being tied down with a multitude of administrative details, will be charged with helping staff to develop the curricular programs needed by students. It will be the I. C. who will work most closely with teachers in helping them to be better performers in the classroom. But what the Instructional Consultant does or does not do is determined by the building principal.

In this day and age, successful administrators rely heavily upon advisors in helping them to consider many different factors prior to making a final decision. The Instructional Consultant serves as such an advisor to the three other members of the leadership team—the building principal, the Pupil Personnel Consultant, and the Coordinator of Independent Study and Student Research. He informs the building principal about the instructional programs being developed, the teaching techniques being employed, the problems being encountered, and the needs of individual teachers and teams. The I. C. advises the guidance staff about students that he has observed in the classroom setting, and makes recommendations about matching teams and students. The I. C. also works closely with the independent study coordinator in the evaluation of student research and in diagnosing student preparedness for such undertakings.

For the Instructional Consultant to play such a vital and essential role in the middle school, the building principal must be a very secure individual, and not so concerned with his own image that he will not let another take the play away from him in certain areas. The I. C. must have the complete confidence and support of his principal if he is to succeed. If the principal is afraid that he will be surpassed by a dynamic, progressive Instructional Consultant, and therefore treats the I. C. as just another subordinate, the progress of the organization will be greatly handicapped. Thus the more freedom and responsibility the I. C. is given, the better he can educate, advise, stimulate, and innovate.

It must be understood that the Instructional Consultant, along with the building principal, the Pupil Personnel Consultant, and the Coordinator of Independent Study and Student Research, are all working together to coordinate the primary activities of the building. Their unified goal is to create an atmosphere of mutual understanding and cooperation among the staff so that each student will receive the type of program he needs.

The I. C. and the Teachers

As was indicated previously, the Instructional Consultant is the member of the building leadership team who will work most closely with teachers on a daily basis. His job is to help all members of the staff to grow professionally. To accomplish this he must not present a threat to those with whom he works. This means that the I. C. must employ his powers of persuasion to influence teacher behavior. He must help others to decide to change, but he must not force them to do so. To do this the I. C. must be flexible, amenable to change himself, and willing to follow the suggestions of others.

From the teachers' point of view, the I. C. must be a human resource, a wellspring of suggestions, a sounding board for their own ideas. He must be a source of encouragement, a supporter, an individual willing to work closely with them on a moment's notice. If they need some materials to accomplish a particular goal, he must be able to secure them, or know where to get them. He must be a teacher's teacher, always willing to help.

By acting in this way the Instructional Consultant should be able to establish rapport with staff and gradually, as his competence is acknowledged and his honesty and integrity are taken for granted, he will begin to be viewed as a helping teacher and as a master teacher.

Once rapport has been established, the I. C. can better work with individual teachers in helping them to comprehend the philosophy of the middle school and some of its anticipated operational procedures. Discussions between the Instructional Consultant and teachers should thoroughly explore such topics as:

1. How the teacher can *individualize* his *instruction* to meet the needs of different students.

2. Forming appropriate instructional groupings by taking advantage of the opportunities presented by an *ungraded* approach to grouping and instruction.

3. Diagnostic techniques to be utilized to identify students capable of pursuing *independent study*.

4. *Continuous* student *progress*. This concept demands that the teacher be aware of the background and educational experience of each of his students. Once this is known, the teacher can then develop specific programs that will permit each student to progress in a manner well suited to his learning style.

It is vital to the success of the middle school that each member of the staff comprehend what is meant by individualized instruction, ungradedness, independent study, and continuous progress. Such an understanding will not be reached after one meeting. The dialogue between each teacher and the I. C. must be a continual one. Patience must prevail. The consultant must realize and appreciate the particular biases and prejudices that each teacher brings to the situation as well as his own preconceived notions. Knowing these, he must work from that point on and hope that his arguments for change, for understanding, and for applicability will eventually have some effect on the individual teacher.

It is also the Instructional Consultant's responsibility to help individual teachers in:

1. The creation of pretesting vehicles to be used as a basis for program development.

2. Planning units designed to help students acquire specific skills or grasp certain concepts.

3. Varying their methods of instruction to coincide with the different learning styles of their students.

4. The development of different evaluative techniques designed to measure both student growth and teacher effectiveness.

The I. C. should not openly criticize all that has previously existed in the field of education because some of what has been done was good, though perhaps not as appropriate today as it once was. He must instead help staff to value change. He must help teachers to de-emphasize the past and devote more time and energy to the present and the future. The I. C. must cause teachers to realize that the middle school is a place where students can and should grow and change as complete individuals. He, along with the other members of the building leadership team, must convince the staff that they can no longer afford to resist and deplore change.

It has not been unusual for teachers to insist that things be done only their way; that way, in the mind of the teacher, was synonymous with the correct way. Such a viewpoint naturally suppressed student creativity, thus counteracting the whole purpose of education. Many modern educational theorists agree with Piaget when he states that

> The principal goal of education . . . is to create men who are capable of doing new things, not simply of repeating what other generations have done—men who are creative, inventive and discoverers. The second goal of education is to form minds which can be critical, can verify, and not accept everything they are offered. The great danger today is of slogans, collective opinions, ready-made trends of thought. We have to be able to resist individually, to criticize, to distinguish between what is proven and what is not. So we need pupils who are active, who learn early to find out by themselves, partly by their own spontaneous activity and partly through materials we set up for them; who learn early to tell what is verifiable and what is simply the first idea to come to them.[2]

If however teachers are to be expected to implement this philosophy and to value change, they must see that the leadership team itself must

2. Jean Piaget as quoted by David Elkind, "Giant in the Nursery—Jean Piaget," *The New York Times Magazine,* May 26, 1968, p. 80. © 1968 by The New York Times Company. Reprinted by permission.

value change and will support those who attempt the new, provided that the innovators have a valid reason for each undertaking and are willing to honestly evaluate each endeavor. To achieve this lofty, but essential goal, the I. C. will have to make it clear to staff that changes will only occur in an environment where individuals value change, where differences are appreciated and not just tolerated, and where occasional mistakes are accepted as part of the natural process of experimentation. Therefore it is essential that there be constant communication between the Instructional Consultant and each teacher to clarify these points.

Helping the Beginning Teacher

Since an ungraded middle school organized on an interdisciplinary teaming basis demands far more of teachers than is usually required of them in a traditionally organized junior high school setting, great care must be taken to properly orient new teachers.

The Instructional Consultant must be involved in recruitment and hiring where his opinion, along with those of the teachers and the building principal, determines who will be recommended for employment. He must also help each new teacher to establish realistic goals for himself and for his students. This can only take place when the neophyte adopts a basic philosophy of education and comprehends its implications for classroom procedures. Once the individual has this clearly in mind, and when this has been conveyed to and understood by the I. C., then both can work together to achieve mutually agreed upon goals.

There are many areas of concern to a beginning teacher. If these doubts and areas of confusion are not alleviated as quickly as possible, it can be a disastrous experience for both students and teacher. The I. C. must elicit from the new teacher what his concerns are. This means that the advisor must be prepared to discuss topics that may often seem, to an experienced observer, to be petty and superficial. The I. C. cannot afford to take such an approach. He must have empathy for the teacher and his concern, realizing that the problem is very important to that individual teacher. Thus topics often explored with a new teacher include:

1. How to make use of different audio-visual equipment;
2. What should be done in the homeroom period;
3. How to take attendance;
4. How to handle rude students;
5. How to get assignments passed out and collected efficiently;
6. How often quizzes should be given;
7. Whether to let students go to the lavatory whenever they want; and
8. What the principal is looking for when he visits a class.

By exploring these topics in depth with the teacher in a relaxed, nonthreatening environment, the I. C. should enable him to gain self-confidence. In addition to exploring problems or concerns raised by the teacher, the Instructional Consultant should in turn bring up topics that the teacher should be concerned about, but of which he may not be initially aware. Two such areas are testing and test construction as well as the selection of textbooks and other reading materials.

For the new teacher, with his limited student teaching experience, it appears to be easy to develop a quiz or a test. But if the teacher is at all astute, he will begin to notice, both from the results as well as from student comments, that some quizzes are too hard while others are too easy. The new teacher may also find that he tends to use one type of question to the exclusion of others to elicit student responses. Both of these situations should be discussed with the I. C.

The Instructional Consultant should pursue with the teacher his purpose in testing. Is it just to give a grade? Is it to determine how much the student has learned? Is it to estimate how effective the teacher has been? Each teacher must be led to reflect on his reasons for testing and on the vehicles he is employing to achieve his goals. Is the teacher using:

1. Fill in the blanks;
2. True-false;
3. Multiple choice;
4. Matching column;
5. Essay; or
6. Verbal explanatory questions?

In these conferences with new teachers, the Instructional Consultant should stress what should be the two primary purposes of testing, namely:

1. To cause each student to draw together the main ideas and the significant details of the topic studied, to relate these main ideas and details to what has been learned before, and to apply them to new situations. This causes each pupil to give evidence of the extent of his mastery of the basic concepts of the unit studied, and his understanding of the relationship of these concepts to his previous learning.

2. To evaluate what a student knows or does not know for the purpose of helping the student in future classes to learn what he has not mastered and, if he gives evidence of mastery, to continue his progress unimpeded by the needless repetition of what he has previously learned.[3]

Reading is a problem area for many teachers, especially for those new to the profession. During the course of the year the perceptive

---

3. Robert J. McCarthy, *How to Organize and Operate an Ungraded Middle School* (Englewood Cliffs, New Jersey: Prentice-Hall, Inc., 1967), p. 44.

teacher will usually notice that some students cannot read or comprehend the textbook material, while others are bored by the same material. The beginning teacher, who generally has little or no training in the field of reading, does not know how to cope with this situation. The teacher usually finds himself with a set of textbooks, or if the district is a forward looking one, a variety of texts, both hard-cover editions and paperbacks. Thus there are students and there are reading materials present in the classroom, but they do not appear to be well suited to each other. This is where the I. C. must play an important role in the education of the new teacher.

The Instructional Consultant must aid the teacher in fully comprehending the notion that the single textbook, single assignment approach is the antithesis of the individualization and personalization of instruction, which is an integral part of the middle school's philosophy. Once this is understood, the teacher will hopefully begin to realize that a variety of sources, including films, filmstrips, slides, tapes, and records, as well as printed material, will have to be employed for him to be effective with different students. This means that audio-visual materials as well as different textbooks and paperbacks, along with teacher-prepared materials, will have to be present and available for student use.

The problem of what specific reading materials to select for each student and on what basis they should be chosen still has to be settled by the I. C. and the teacher. It must be emphasized by the Instructional Consultant that the readability level as well as the interest level of the printed material must be appropriate for each student if success is to be achieved.

Two things must therefore be done prior to selecting printed materials. To begin with, the teacher must determine the general reading level of the students either by examining their pupil personnel records or by giving them a diagnostic reading test. If the teacher does not feel confident enough to administer such a test, arrangements should be made with the school's reading teacher to give it. Once the teacher has gotten a reading score on each student, then he can begin to examine printed matter to see if the material is too easy, too difficult, or appropriate for the student. But a teacher cannot simply glance at a textbook or paperback and tell, with any degree of accuracy, the reading difficulty of the material from a student's point of view. There are however several accepted formulas that can be used to make such determinations.

One such method has been developed by Rudolf Flesch. It has proven to be of great benefit to teachers. Figures 5-A and 5-B illustrate material prepared by Raymond F. Stopper, Jr., a former Instructional Consultant with the Liverpool Central School District, Liverpool, New

York, to introduce staff to the practice of analyzing classroom reading material. As an I. C. in the Liverpool Middle School, Mr. Stopper helped staff to use Flesch's Readability Formula to great advantage in analyzing printed matter.

Figure 5-C describes another technique that can be used with staff to help them determine the suitability of their reading material for different students.

Working with Teams

When teachers are working in teams and no longer isolated in their self-contained classrooms, planning takes on new dimensions. The thoughts and ideas of each team member are brought out into the open where they can be scrutinized by a number of individuals. For many teachers these are entirely new working conditions. Some are frightened by them and must be helped to realize that such an atmosphere can be of great benefit to all concerned if proper use is made of the setting. All can grow by watching and being watched by one's colleagues, if the observations are positively oriented.

To: Staff
From: Ray Stopper
Re: Flesch's Readability Formula

In answer to several requests by teachers, I am forwarding to you at this time material pertaining to the Flesch readability formula. This formula is in reality a procedure for determining the ease or difficulty which an individual student is likely to encounter with materials that you, the teacher, expect him to read.

These techniques produce *gross* indications of the grade or difficulty levels of the matter. One team recently discovered that the passage they selected at random in a so-called "sixth-grade" science textbook was actually appropriate for a student with an "eighth-grade" reading ability. Some "seventh-grade" textbooks have materials in them with a readability level as high as twelfth grade.

If any staff member is interested in *how* a teacher *untrained* in reading can help his students to read successfully in his own subject matter area, please see me as soon as possible. Films are also available at the present time in my office for your use in which interesting and productive techniques for helping students to read material in science, social studies, etc., are explained in detail and demonstrated.

Figure 5–A

Memo from I. C. to Staff on
the Flesch Readability Formula

FLESCH'S READABILITY FORMULA[4]

I. *Major Steps in this technique:*

1. Select one to three representative paragraphs in the book, excluding introductory paragraphs.
2. Count up to 100 words.
3. Find the average length of each sentence.
4. Find the number of syllables per 100 words.

II. *Formula:*

1. Multiply the average sentence length by 1.015   _____
2. Multyply the number of syllables per 100 words by .846   _____
3. Find the sum of 1 and 2   _____
4. Subtract this sum (#3) from 206.835   _____
5. The net result is the reading ease score   _____

III. *Grade Equivalents:*

90-100	4th Grade
80-90	5th Grade
70-80	6th Grade
60-70	7th or 8th Grade
50-60	Some high school
30-50	High school or some College
0-30	College

IV. *Other Interpretations:*

			Number of Syllables	Length of Sentence
90-100	Very easy	Comics	123 per 100	8 words
80-90	Easy	Pulp Fiction	131 ” ”	11 words
70-80	Fairly Easy	Slick Fiction	139 ” ”	14 words
60-70	Standard	Digests, *Time*	147 ” ”	17 words
50-60	Fairly Diff.	*Harper's*	155 ” ”	21 words
30-50	Difficult	Academic	167 ” ”	25 words
0-30	Very Diff.	Scientific	192 ” ”	29 words

Figure 5–B
Flesch's Readability Formula

---

4. Rudolph Flesch, *How to Test Readability,* pp. 1-6, 44. ©1951, by Rudolph Flesch. Reprinted by permission of Harper & Row, Publishers, Inc.

To: Staff
From: Ray Stopper
Re: The Cloze Readability Procedure.

The cloze procedure is another method that can be used to determine each student's ability to read the material that the teacher is asking him to read. It involves seven basic steps:[5]

1. Select three passages of 250 words each from three different sections of the book. These passages should be *representative* of the kind of material that you expect the students to read.

2. Delete every fifth word and replace it with a blank space.

3. Ask the students to supply the missing words. It should be noted that:

    A. The student should *not* have read beforehand the material from which the passages have been selected;

    B. The exact word only is acceptable; and

    C. There should be no time limit for completing the assignment.

4. If the student is able to provide 57% or more of the missing words, he is probably able to read the material *independently* with little or no assistance.

5. If the student is able to provide between 44% and 57% of the missing words, the material is judged to be at his *instructional* level, which means that he will require *some assistance* in order to read the material successfully.

6. If the student is able to supply *fewer* than 44% of the missing words, the material is probably at his *frustration* level, and you should look for other sources from which the student can learn, such as books at an easier reading level, discussions with fellow pupils, or the same material recorded on tape. It should be recalled that a student's listening comprehension is usually one to two or more grade levels higher than his reading comprehension. Films, filmstrips, and comic books can also be effectively used here.

7. The student's performance with the *three* designated passages should give you a *gross* indication of his capability for reading the material you selected.

I will be happy to work with you in applying the procedure to materials you select.

Figure 5–C
The Cloze Readability Procedure

---

5. John R. Bormuth, "The Cloze Readability Procedure," *Elementary English*, XLV, No. 4 (April, 1968), pp. 429-436, reprinted with the permission of the National Council of Teachers of English and John R. Bormuth.

The Instructional Consultant must work closely with all the teams and with members of the teams as individuals. In practice the I. C. must strive to have himself considered as a participating member and working colleague of all teams. He must serve as a resource person, while at the same time exerting a quiet, effective influence on the teams by his low keyed approach. In this way the Instructional Consultant will enable each team to become a cohesive unit, ready to take full advantage of the opportunities presented by the unique organizational structure of the ungraded middle school.

Since the success or failure of the entire teaming operation hinges on the team planning sessions and on how the individual members of each team work together, the I. C. must:

1. Meet each week with each interdisciplinary and related arts team;
2. Schedule monthly meetings with teachers of the same discipline;
3. Conduct monthly, voluntary in-service faculty meetings on topics suggested by staff;
4. Talk on a regular basis with all members of the staff, particularly new and/or non-tenure teachers;
5. Visit classrooms on a regular basis to be fully aware of what is going on instructionally within the school; and
6. Meet once each week with the other members of the building leadership team to assess the overall progress of the school.

After the I. C. has attended a team's planning session, it is a good idea to see all four members of the team in operation in the classroom sometime during that same week. This can give him a complete picture of the team's functioning. It is suggested that when this is done for the first time, the I. C. meet with each member of the team individually prior to the visitation. At this time the teacher can further inform the I. C. of what he plans to do in a particular class, why he has decided to do this, and how he plans to evaluate it. This is basically an information session for the advisor.

When the visitation is over, and the visit should last as long as the class lasts, the I. C. and the teacher should plan to meet later on in the day to discuss what transpired. At this post-visitation conference 'the I. C. must get the teacher to be the first one to evaluate his effectiveness in the lesson just seen. It is less than desirable to have the advisor begin the session by revealing his own comments and observations. Since the primary purpose of the meeting is to help the teacher grow professionally in order to be more effective, the burden for evaluation must fall on the teacher himself. The I. C. must resist the temptation to lead.

Once the staff member has conveyed his own impressions of the lesson to the I. C., the latter should then share his views, notes, and perceptions of the class just seen. Since no formal evaluative report will be written up by the I. C. about the individual's performance, an environment of trust and openness should be created. This hopefully will lead teams to continually invite this advisor and counselor to observe different classroom situations and share his views of the operation with them. If this three-phase procedure of:

1. Pre-visitation conference,
2. Classroom visitation, and
3. Post-visitation conference is employed successfully every team member should benefit from it.

As the I. C. meets with the teams he should help them to both organize and coordinate their efforts. This can best be done by giving each team some type of procedural guideline to follow as they debate the concepts to possibly be explored or the skills needed to be worked on with specific students. It is recommended that each team:

1. Analyze all available data on each of its students;
2. Establish realistic goals for its students to attain and determine equally realistic objectives for itself as a team;
3. Organize all of its operations so that the goals previously established can be achieved;
4. Implement all procedures needed to reach the stated objectives;
5. Evaluate
   a. Whether or not the objectives were achieved;
   b. How much the pupils grew in the areas stressed;
   c. The effectiveness of the techniques employed; and
   d. How the team functioned as a unit;
6. Make the changes needed in light of the evaluations conducted; and
7. Initiate new plans in view of the analyses of previous operations.

In addition to these guidelines, the Instructional Consultant should work with each team in:

1. Determining the interests, needs, and abilities of its students;
2. Successfully employing diverse instructional techniques specifically designed to help different students acquire the skills necessary to become independent learners;
3. Preparing written summaries of units developed for different youngsters;
4. Helping to insure the students' active, not passive, participation in the learning process;
5. Reviewing material covered in other classes in previous years and building on these skills and concepts; and

6. Discovering new sources of information that can better help the students to learn.

As the I. C. works with each team, he should help it to become more and more independent. As this occurs he will gradually begin to play a different role. He will continually help in curriculum development, serving as a guiding force in this area. It is also his responsibility, when such endeavors are underway, to bring to the team's attention any pertinent research that may have a bearing on their work. When the findings of others who have engaged in related projects are made known to the teachers, much duplication of effort can be avoided. It is this repeated failure to disseminate the findings of others doing research in similar or related project areas that has caused many innovative undertakings to fail in their early developmental stages.

While the Instructional Consultant works in various capacities with all teams, he should enable each one to become a more efficient, productive teaching unit. Helping each team member to work within the flexible framework of the middle school, aiding him in coping with the newness of the team planning sessions and team teaching situations, and causing each team to thoroughly and honestly evaluate its effectiveness with its students is an awesome task, but it must be done if the Instruction Consultant is to be an effective member of the building leadership team.

Relationships with the Building Principal

While the Instructional Consultant is engaged in tasks mentioned in previous sections of this chapter, the building principal is also performing many of these same functions. But because of the demands made upon the office, the principal is not able to give the in-depth guidance necessary to help staff develop a quality instructional program. Therefore it is essential that the principal have complete faith in his Instructional Consultant's ability and judgment in leading teachers.

The I. C. must in turn have confidence in his principal. He must share his thoughts and observations with him, but at the same time must be free to withhold certain confidential matters which, if disclosed, would adversely affect his rapport with teachers. For example, if the I. C. is working with a teacher on a problem and seems to be resolving it, there is no need for him to discuss the matter with the principal. If however the situation is not improving or seems to be getting worse, the I. C. should ask for the principal's view of it.

Occasionally there may also be a case where a teacher may be critical of the principal's operations. If the I. C. cannot get the individual teacher to discuss the matter personally with the principal (the best way to resolve the issue), he might choose to discuss it in a general way with the principal, not revealing the name of the teacher who raised the point.

The I. C. is only an advisor. He possesses no authority. He writes no supervisory reports. It is the principal who is the authority figure and who writes evaluative reports on teaching personnel based on his own classroom observations. Thus when advised of a situation that needs improvement, the principal can play the "heavy" when this is the only way to get a teacher to change his behavior. In reality, the building principal can enforce what is suggested by the I. C. This however should seldom be done, except in emergency situations, otherwise the I. C. could be viewed as an administrative stoolie who "rats" to the principal when his suggestions are not followed. The I. C. must therefore only ask the principal's help as an enforcer when all else has failed.

The I. C. and the principal must work as a unit in helping to improve the entire instructional program. Since an ungraded middle school organized on an interdisciplinary teaming basis with many decision-making prerogatives accorded to staff is a relatively new concept, it is essential that they keep each other appraised of developments within teams. They must complement each other in their professional activities. Since both will work with the entire staff, it is recommended that the two possess different academic backgrounds. This will give the instructional leadership team a much needed balance and diminish the chances of over-emphasizing a curriculum area to the detriment of other important subject matter areas.

Both the building principal and the Instructional Consultant, working together, can strive to overcome the handicaps that have, in the past, stifled many of the creative endeavors undertaken by staff. As the I. C. works closely with teachers and teams and unearths new plans for the improvement of the instructional program, the principal must find ways and create situations where these ideas can be tested.

While it is expected that both the I. C. and the principal will work in harmony, there will have to be times when disagreements about decisions to be made or strategies to be employed will arise. Both must seek to understand the position of the other. This can only come about through honest, open dialogue. At times the I. C. must yield to the principal's point of view, and at times the principal must acquiesce. For example, the building principal may occasionally have to temper the enthusiasm of an I. C. who is advocating an idea suggested by a teacher because of the adverse effects it may have. In fulfilling their responsibilities both men must seek to maintain the delicate balance between the challenge to be creative and the accountability for the results produced.

There will be times when the decision should not be made until aired with the entire leadership team. But since the principal has the ultimate responsibility for the total operations of the building, whatever decision is arrived at becomes his decision. Thus there will be occasions when he will overrule the I. C. This is the nature of his position. But if this occurs frequently, something is very wrong within the leadership team itself, and must be analyzed and corrected immediately.

To a large extent the success of the middle school will be determined by how well the Instructional Consultant and the principal work together.

The I. C. and Central Office Personnel

If the district is large enough to have several middle schools, the consultants should form an instructional council under the leadership of the assistant superintendent for instructional services. Formal meetings should be held at least once a month at which time the instructional consultants discuss common problems and areas of concern with the assistant superintendent and the director of secondary education, if there is one.

In districts that have instructional consultants in all buildings, both elementary and secondary, monthly meetings should be held with the assistant superintendent for instructional services, the director of elementary education, and the director of secondary education. Topics discussed at these sessions should pertain to the entire district and help to improve the articulation necessary to insure the students' continuous progress on a K-12 basis. Badly needed in-service programs can be planned during the course of these meetings.

Periodically central office personnel should visit the school and talk with the entire leadership team as a unit, and individually with its different members. This will afford the I. C. an excellent opportunity to show the visitors what is taking place instructionally within the school, and thus boost staff morale.

A Typical Working Schedule

The best way to fully comprehend the vital role that the Instructional Consultant plays in the middle school is to examine his schedule over a two-day span.

First Day

7:00 A.M.   receives calls from teachers who are ill. He then contacts available substitutes.

8:00 A.M.   arrives at school. He sees to it that audio-visual material requested by staff has been distributed by the teacher aides.

8:30 A.M.	welcomes substitute teachers, gives them the emergency lesson plans, and introduces them to the team.
9:00 A.M.	travels throughout the building, pausing to visit with teachers along his route.
9:15 A.M.	joins the principal for coffee and a discussion of what transpired at the previous evening's board of education meeting.
9:45 A.M.	pre-visitation conference with a teacher.
10:30 A.M.	meets with the Coordinator of Independent Study and Student Research to discuss a particular student's proposal.
11:00 A.M.	classroom visitation.
11:30 A.M.	has lunch with several staff members in the faculty dining room.
12:00 M.	visits with students in the library and learning centers.
12:15 P.M.	post-visitation conference with the teacher.
1:00 P.M.	meets with the Reading teacher to talk about how reading problems are being handled in the various content areas.
1:30 P.M.	talks with the building principal and the Reading teacher about the school's reading program and how different teams are handling it.
2:00 P.M.	attends a team planning session.
2:45 P.M.	sees all substitute teachers as they leave and secures from them their perceptions of the day.
3:05 P.M.	meets with the foreign language teachers to discuss the ALM approach to instruction as well as alternative programs.
4:15 P.M.	catches up on some professional reading.
4:45 P.M.	sees the principal about tomorrow's field trip and the scheduled interview with a candidate for a teaching position.
5:00 P.M.	heads for home.

Second Day

8:15 A.M.	arrives at school. He sees to it that the teacher aides have typed and run off materials needed by the staff.
8:45 A.M.	tours the school, visiting with teachers along the way.
9:00 A.M.	meets with the guidance counselors to discuss the team placement of several new pupils.
9:30 A.M.	pre-visitation conference.
10:00 A.M.	classroom visitation.
10:45 A.M.	sees to it that the field trip gets underway smoothly.

11:15 A.M.   post-visitation conference.

11:45 A.M.   has lunch with the principal to discuss the professional growth of the two teachers recently observed and the total operations of their team.

12:15 P.M.   meets briefly with the candidate for the teaching position and introduces her to the team that will have the vacancy.

12:45 P.M.   attends a meeting of the Middle School Instructional Council. Those in attendance are the assistant superintendent for instruction, the director of secondary education, and the instructional consultants from the other middle schools in the district.

2:15 P.M.   meets with the building principal and the interdisciplinary team that interviewed the teacher candidate to make a decision regarding her employment.

3:00 P.M.   talks with teachers on an informal basis as they leave the building.

3:45 P.M.   professional reading and correspondence.

4:30 P.M.   end of day.

Just a casual glance at the tasks he performs, including the vital one of securing the necessary substitutes who will work well in teaming situations, indicates the awesome demands made upon the individual occupying the position of Instructional Consultant. He must in reality be a jack-of-all-trades and a master of management diplomacy to fulfill his duties and responsibilities.

Summary

The Instructional Consultant can have the greatest impact on the school's instructional program because of the very nature of his duties and responsibilities. As chief advisor and counselor of teachers, he alone has sufficient time and freedom to work with staff in helping them to fulfill the new demands made by the ungraded middle school.

He must not only be able to relate to new and experienced teachers, but also to different teaching teams as they encounter challenges posed by an interdisciplinary approach to individualized instruction. Because he deals mainly with people, the quality of his relationships with the building principal, as well as with other members of the leadership team and central office personnel, will go far in determining the goals that will be achieved in the undertaking.

As an analysis of the Instructional Consultant's daily work load indicates, he holds the key position in the school's attempt to develop quality educational programs well suited to early adolescents.

Chapter 6

Independent Study for
the Middle School Years

IT IS DIFFICULT for any educator who has spent a number of
years in traditionally oriented schools and districts to detach
himself from what has become the accepted thing. The very idea of
allowing students to work on their own, without direct teacher supervision, outside the confines of the classroom, is thought by many to be
unworkable, if not dangerous, especially for early adolescents. Such
prevailing viewpoints have caused many teachers and administrators to
look with skepticism at independent study.

This chapter will define what is meant by independent study and will
clarify the definition with specific examples. Criteria established for
pursuing independent study programs and the use of pretests as well as
other devices to ascertain student interest in such undertakings will be
explored along with the necessity for a coordinator to supervise the entire
operation. The coordinator's duties and responsibilities, his relationships
with the staff and with the students, will be analyzed along with forms
and procedures that might possibly be used to evaluate student research.
A method of judging the total effectiveness of independent study
programs in the middle school will also be presented.

Independent Study Defined

Independent study for youngsters of middle school age should be defined as that instructional technique which "capitalizes on the student's interest in a particular area by allowing the youngster to pursue research outside the confines of the classroom."[1] The project undertaken may be directly related to the topic being explored with the other students in the class or it may be in an entirely different area.

The impetus for independent study must be the motivation of the individual student himself. The reward is basically one of self-fulfillment. Thus independent study is not, and cannot be, solely a teacher initiated and directed assignment. While the teacher or other members of the staff may act as resources and encouragers of the students, they are not the prime movers in the endeavor. The student himself must supply that vital force. He determines the subject matter of his research study. The curriculum currently being studied may supply the inspiration for the research project, but it must not dictate it.

Since the ungraded middle school is committed to developing appropriate, individualized instructional programs for its students to help them become independent learners, a variety of procedures and approaches have to be used to achieve this goal. An independent study program is one such method. A continuous progress approach to education, an integral part of the middle school philosophy, also demands that opportunities be present for students to pursue independent study programs. An independent study program thus presents students with a framework within which they can move at their own pace in accordance with their abilities, should they choose to take advantage of the opportunities offered by this approach.

While innumerable activities have recently been classified as independent study programs in an attempt to get on a current educational bandwagon, true independent study programs must, in this author's professional opinion, meet the following criteria:

1. The student selects his own research topic.
2. The selection is followed by teacher-student planning to clarify the goals of the project.
3. For the duration of the research study, students are excused from attending regularly scheduled classes and are not held responsible for tests, quizzes, and homework assignments in the discipline in which the research is being conducted. The student however may occasionally be asked to attend the class on a specific day when an important presentation is being made.
4. Sufficient time is given to complete the study.

---

1. Robert J. McCarthy, *How to Organize and Operate an Ungraded Middle School* (Englewood Cliffs, New Jersey: Prentice-Hall, Inc., 1967), p. 49.

5. The research can be carried on either in school facilities or elsewhere if necessary as agreed upon by the student and the staff members involved.
6. The work completed is accepted in lieu of the class work done by the other students.
7. Evaluation of the independent study project involves the student and members of the staff.

Programs that meet these specifications allow students and staff to depart from the usual curriculum patterns. They give both an opportunity to explore a variety of ways to tap many different resources, enabling youngsters, some for the first time, to grasp fundamental research skills while at the same time comprehending certain basic concepts.

Initiation of Specific Independent Study Programs

A pupil may arrive at a decision to pursue independent study in a variety of ways. If for example his social studies teacher happens to be exploring principles of economics with his group, the youngster might express a desire to explore the basic operations of the stock market. His teacher then makes the necessary arrangements that would allow him to undertake the research. Perhaps the student is interested in this topic because his father works for a brokerage firm or plays the market, or because he listened to news broadcasts and the conversations of others. Knowing that the school provides means for pursuing research in such areas because the entire independent study program has been explained to him and his classmates on several occasions, the student asks the teacher if he can undertake a research study dealing with the stock market.

The teacher and the student would then sit down and discuss the nature of the proposed study. The discussion should help the student to clarify his objectives, limit the scope of his research, and comtemplate different methods of investigation. If after such a discussion the teacher decides that the proposed project would be of benefit to the student, then the youngster is allowed to pursue his research instead of attending his regularly scheduled social studies classes. The role of the Coordinator of Independent Study and Student Research in the undertaking will be explored later on in this chapter.

In another related instance centering on some basic principles of economics, a student in a Social Studies group who is interested in both Home and Consumer Economics might wonder why various cake mixes are priced differently. After discussing this with both her Social Studies and Home Economics teachers, the student would then purchase several different brands, noting differences not only in cost, but also in the ingredients contained in each. She then might bake identical cakes, following the recipe on each box, comparing baking times, etc., plus additional ingredients that had to be added to each cake and the cost of each item. Classmates could sample the cakes and rate them. The student's findings could then be summarized in a comparison chart and shown to several classes in Social Studies and Home Economics.

It is also likely that, with some shy middle school students, independent study research projects will be initiated through subtle teacher suggestions. From classroom as well as personal observations, a teacher might notice that, although a particular student appears to be quite capable of undertaking a research project and has shown definite interest in several topics that have recently been discussed, the student seems hesitant about undertaking independent study. The teacher might speak to the youngster in an informal setting, further inquire about his interests, suggest that he initiate an independent study program to satisfy these interests, and see what happens. But the teacher must be patient. He must encourage, wait, see, and resist the temptation to push.

Quite often in the process of class discussions a student will ask a worthwhile question requiring an in-depth answer. The teacher may not feel it is appropriate to go into the topic with the entire group. He may instead suggest to the student that it may be to his advantage to answer his own question through independent study. A teacher must be careful however that he does not use this method indiscriminately and thus discourage students from asking questions. Most questions should most certainly be answered on the spot.

It must be understood that simply doing a term paper, even on a student selected topic, is not independent study. Independent study must not be connected in any way with a uniform type of assignment to a significant portion of students in a class. Thus there is a definite difference in this author's opinion between independent study and studying independently. The former calls for student initiative and possible departures from normal courses of study. The latter, while certainly a vital part of the educational process, may be very much teacher directed and call for little imaginative, creative work on the part of the student.

Criteria for Pursuing Independent Study

The three criteria that must be met before a student should be permitted to participate in an independent study undertaking are:

1. The student must demonstrate genuine interest in a particular project.

2. The proposed research must be beneficial to the youngster.

3. The pupil must be able to function with a considerable degree of success while working outside of the typical classroom structure for a period of time.

All students, regardless of their ability, must be considered as potential candidates for independent study since one of the essential prerequisites for participation is interest. Any student, irrespective of his ability, has certain areas of interest and thus can fulfill at least one of the criteria for entrance into the program.. When such interest is demonstrated, the teacher must encourage the student to pursue it. Once again it cannot be stressed too emphatically that teacher-selected topics assigned to different students which necessitate considerable out of class time to complete are not to be considered as independent study research projects. Such an approach to the concept of independent study is the antithesis of the basic idea underlying the program. Independent study is more than just working on one's own. It is the student working on his own, with minimal adult guidance and supervision, on a topic of his own choosing.

When teachers treat independent study programs as teacher-directed and teacher-controlled assignments, with the students still held responsible for work covered in class and the accompanying tests and quizzes, it becomes very clear to the students that they are merely doing extra work. The idea of a youngster pursuing research to satisfy his curiosity disappears and is replaced by the "give the teacher what he wants" kind of attitude that prevails today throughout much of education. This generally creates situations where only those pupils who are very highly motivated or those who desperately need extra points to pass a course will participate in such "extra credit" projects.

The second criteria that must be met before the student should be allowed to undertake independent study concerns the benefits that the research will have for the individual. This can only be determined by the teacher and the pupil after they have discussed the proposed study. The student may have certain goals that he wishes to achieve. The teacher may have different ones. Both points of view should be analyzed. Then realistic expectations can be established.

Other benefits, aside from the uncovering of important facts or the supporting evidence for a theory, can accrue to the student as a result of independent study. Students usually see independent study as a way of acquiring information on a topic of interest to them. The teacher and the coordinator must not however have such a limited view but must be able to see that certain behavioral and operational benefits can result from the research which may have long-range, positive effects on the students. The self-confidence that the youngster begins to acquire as a result of searching something out on his own may be more beneficial to him than the actual importance of the information uncovered. The feeling that the school trusts the student enough to allow him to pursue his interest area instead of attending a certain class is an attitude that, when present, may alter the youngster's view of the school and of education. The pride that a student feels when allowed to participate in a special program is another important consideration that may well be a basis for allowing him to pursue independent study.

Discussions between pupil and teacher to discover whether the research will benefit the student quickly uncover proposals that are merely whims, passing fancies, or an attempt to get out of a regularly scheduled class. These certainly would not be valid reasons for pursuing any study and would prevent the student from participating in the program at that time because he failed to meet one of the criteria— genuine interest in a topic.

The third criteria for allowing a pupil to begin an independent study program requires that he be judged capable of working in a structure completely severed from the normal classroom setting. If the teacher, the team, or the coordinator determines that he cannot function effectively in such a setting the student would be excluded from the formal independent study program at that time. It would mean that his teachers and his team would have to work more closely with him in preparing him for working in such an environment in the future.

Students meeting these three criteria should be permitted to undertake independent study research projects. This has immediate significance for the student and his teachers. It indicates that the youngster is not expected to pursue the same curricular program as many of his classmates. His own unique individualized program has been developed for him because of an interest that he himself has expressed. This is certainly a logical way to develop curriculum, especially in a middle school that seeks to create individualized instructional programs. As Paul Goodman has stated: "It seems stupid to decide a priori what the young ought to know and then try to motivate them, instead of letting the initiative come from them and putting information and relevant equipment at their service."[2]

Ascertaining Student Interests

Interdisciplinary teaming makes it relatively easy to determine student interests. Since close bonds and relationships are established between the students and the teachers on their team, each gets to know the other better. In the classroom, during informal discussions in the

2. Paul Goodman, "Freedom and Learning: the Need for Choice," *Saturday Review,* May 18, 1968, p. 73.

student commons, in the learning centers, and in team planning sessions, teachers begin to get a more complete picture of their students as human beings. If teachers will remain silent and listen, listen attentively to their students, the youngsters will convey very definite messages to them about their interest areas. Combining this data with other impressions of the youngster gathered from the total school environment can indicate to staff those individuals who might be willing to undertake independent study in a particular area under the right conditions.

Pretesting devices can also be used to identify those pupils who seem to have a firm grasp of the skills and concepts that are going to be developed in a forthcoming unit. Once the teacher realizes this and the fact is brought home to the students, at least two alternatives are immediately available to him. He can develop a new topic for study that will both challenge and interest these students or he can allow them to embark on independent study programs if they express a desire to do so. The teacher must be prepared to implement several alternatives simultaneously.

While pretests often reveal certain facts and can provide the teachers with vital data for planning future instructional programs, the key to becoming aware of student interests is to take the time to listen to them. This is achieved by having the teacher, through conscious effort on his part, play a far less dominate role. By posing questions that call more for thought and expression from pupils than for short, crisp factual responses, students will begin to open up.

Thus if the school fosters student-teacher interaction and cooperation, and each begins to understand and appreciate the true role of the other, students will not hesitate to make known their interests. Teachers will then not hesitate to allow their pupils to pursue their interests if organized procedures have been set up to handle such programs.

The Need for a Coordinator

It has become apparent through the years that change in education will not take place by employing conventional approaches within the confines of traditionally organized structures. It is also obvious that if you ask too much of individuals at any one time, disaster results.

Since an ungraded middle school as described in this book demands much of staff in terms of interdisciplinary team planning and teaching in an attempt to individualize instructional programs, and since much of this is very new to the profession, it would be unrealistic to expect staff to launch an independent study program without assistance. While many teachers might realize the necessity for initiating such research proposals with their students, with all the other new demands being made on them, they might hesitate to encourage students to pursue such undertakings if someone were not available to coordinate and supervise these activities; thus the need for a Coordinator of Independent Study and Student Research.

Realizing that the success of the independent study approach to individualized instruction "depends very largely on attitudes of individual instructors toward it, and on the relative importance the faculty and student body attach to independent study and reading,"[3] an individual should be selected to fill this position who has won the respect of both students and staff. Considering the age levels and maturity ranges of middle school students, the coordinator, analyzing his counselees, must give each the minimum of appropriate guidance and supervision. If such is not provided, the student may find himself in serious difficulties with the research, lose self-confidence, refuse to go out again on his own to pursue an interest area, and revert back to his former role as a teacher-dependent pupil.

The key to the success of the middle school will be decided to a large extent by how staff is organized to implement the educational program. There must also be supervision and evaluation of any new instructional programs. This means that time, money, and manpower must be available to accomplish these tasks. No school seriously contemplating allowing its students unlimited opportunities to engage in research studies in areas of their own choosing can afford not to employ a coordinator for the program. This individual's sole responsibility should be that of working with teachers and students on various independent study research proposals.

The position of Coordinator of Independent Study and Student Research is unique. As the school year begins he has no students assigned to him, yet it is conceivable that, during the course of the year, he will be working with a significant number of them. He is not a member of any specific teaching team but he will probably be dealing with all of the teams during the year. Thus for any school just moving into the area of independent study, it is strongly recommended that a coordinator be hired, or preferably selected from the existing staff, to help plan, coordinate, and evaluate all efforts associated with independent study.

Duties and Responsibilities of the Coordinator

If the Coordinator of Independent Study and Student Research is to be effective he must:

1. Meet with the building leadership team to discuss how he would

---

3. John Joseph Margarones, *Critical Requirements of Independent Study Based Upon An Analysis of Critical Incidents as Observed and Reported by Students and Instructors* (Doctoral Dissertation, Boston University, 1961), p. 71.

like to function in his role as coordinator. The composition of the student body and faculty along with the political, social, and economic conditions prevailing in the community should influence the manner in which the coordinator develops his role.

2. Talk with individual teachers, interdisciplinary and related arts teams, content teams, university advisors, and colleagues in other districts to get their views on independent study.

3. Develop a position paper explaining the full scope of the independent study program for distribution to parents and teachers, followed by a series of orientation meetings for teachers, students, and parents.

4. Read widely in the area and become familiar with all research reports dealing with various types of independent study programs.

5. Attend a team planning session of each team at least once a month to determine the different topics that are being developed within each team.

6. Work with staff in developing the appropriate forms and procedures necessary for the smooth operation and evaluation of the program.

7. Help teachers develop specific pretesting devices.

8. Meet with those members of the staff who have students who are interested in undertaking an independent study project. Once this is done, the coordinator should then familarize himself with all the information that the school has on the individual student involved. Then realistic student goals and teacher expectations can be intelligently discussed and agreed upon.

9. Assist students in developing basic research skills, especially the efficient use of time and resources.

10. Develop a system which provides students with daily feedback concerning their progress.

11. Give individual teachers, teams, and guidance counselors weekly progress reports on how their pupils are doing. These reports need not be written but, in the interests of time and efficiency, should be made verbally.

12. Inform the teacher when it appears as if a student's study has been completed or when it seems as if it would be more beneficial for the youngster to return to the regularly scheduled class even though his project may not be completed.

13. Evaluate the student's research study in concert with the student and his teacher.

14. Meet at least once a month with the building leadership team for the expressed purpose of keeping its members informed of the program's

operation. A brief written report should be filed every quarter with the building principal and the Instructional Consultant.

15. Apprise central office personnel, especially the assistant superintendent for instructional services and the director of secondary education, as well as members of the district's Instructional Council, of what is taking place in his school in the area of independent study.

16. Compile a comprehensive report at the conclusion of the school year tallying all studies initiated, completed, and terminated before completion, along with student and faculty observations on the program, for distribution to all interested parties. Outstanding examples of independent study research projects could possibly be gathered together and published in booklet form by the district.

Aside from working with teachers and keeping them informed of program developments, the coordinator's chief task consists of meeting frequently with students involved in the program. These informal sessions can further help the individual student to clarify his research goals and decide upon those techniques that he wishes to use in his study. These conferences will also aid the youngster in preparing his final report and in evaluating it in terms of the previously agreed upon standards.

The coordinator's success in fulfilling his duties and responsibilities will depend greatly on the cooperation of staff as well as other outside agencies. Since school facilities and resources are generally limited in scope, it is essential that the coordinator develop close working relationships with public libraries, neighboring university research facilities, museums, computer centers, business schools, historical societies, and other special interest groups so that his students will have many different resources to use in their research.

Relationships with Staff and Students

In order to win complete support for the program from the entire staff a concerted effort should be made by the coordinator, as well as by the other members of the building leadership team, to explore all facets of independent study with all teachers. Candidates being interviewed to fill existing vacancies should be asked to give their own definition of independent study and to state their views on it. A position should not be offered to anyone who is basically opposed to this approach to education.

Once the new teacher is hired, he should spend time during the summer orientation program with the coordinator. During these discussions the coordinator can, in a relaxed, informal setting, explain to the new staff members why the position of Coordinator of Independent Study and Student Research was created, the scope of his duties and responsibilities, and how he can be of assistance to each of the teachers in helping them to achieve their goals. When all questions raised have been answered in depth and the coordinator feels confident that the new teachers have a firm understanding of his position, then future meetings can be set up with this group to analyze how the program is progressing. In the interim, the coordinator will be working with these teachers on an individual basis.

With experienced staff members the coordinator must use a different approach. Meeting with individual interdisciplinary and related arts teams rather than subject matter teams is probably the most effective way for him to become aware of ways in which he might be of help to the team members and their students. As the year progresses and as teachers are informed of the successes that students have had in undertaking research in particular disciplines, they will be more receptive to allowing the same students, and others like them, to pursue independent study in their own disciplines.

While it is necessary to develop good working relationships with the professional staff, it is also essential that the Coordinator of Independent Study and Student Research establish rapport with students. This will determine the success or failure of the program, for if students fail to respect and get along with the coordinator, they will be reluctant to undertake independent study research projects.

Margarones, in his analysis of the critical requirements for independent study, stressed the importance of "interaction between the student and his advisor."[4] Such interaction should involve "securing cooperation, support, and the encouragement from the advisor; maintaining effective relations with him; implementing suggestions from him; and sharing ideas at regularly held meetings."[5] This requires that the student exhibit a "willingness to be guided and a readiness to learn."[6] The youngster must like the person he is working with and have confidence in him. The Coordinator of Independent Study and Research must therefore create a climate that presents such an attractive image to the students.

The Mechanics of the Program

Once the teacher and the student interested in pursuing independent study determine that the proposed research meets the criteria established for gaining admission to the program, both should complete the first page of the Independent Study Research Proposal, Figure 6-A. Each should

---

4. Margarones, *Critical Requirements of Independent Study Based Upon an Analysis of Critical Incidents as Observed and Reported by Students and Instructors*, p. 157.
5. *Ibid.*
6. *Ibid.*

Independent Study Research Proposal

Pupil's Name: _____ _____
Last   First

Pupil's Age: _____ Year in Middle School: _____

Teacher's Name: _____ Team: _____

Date Project Begun: _____ Date Completed: _____

Student's stetement, in general terms, of the research proposal:

_____
Student's Signature

Teacher's statement concerning the major objectives he hopes the student will achieve from the study:

_____
Teacher's Signature

Figure 6–A

Independent Study Research Proposal—Page 1

state his views of the proposed study and sign his name. The student's signature indicates his willingness to pursue the topic. The teacher's signature indicates his approval of the undertaking and his willingness to allow the student to pursue it instead of regularly attending his class. This form is then submitted by the teacher to the coordinator.

As soon as the coordinator receives the first page of the proposal he should schedule separate meetings with the student and his teacher for the next day. Prior to the meeting he should familiarize himself with all pertinent background information regarding the student. After having first discussed the proposed study with the teacher, the student and the coordinator should sit down in the latter's office and further explore the proposal. The coordinator must draw the student out rather than give him specific directives. He must cause the student to refine his goals, determine specific, realistic objectives, and decide upon possible ways to go about attacking the problem. The advisor must not discourage the student in any way but must encourage him in his efforts. Near the end of the session, the student should write down the specific tasks he wishes to accomplish and how he plans to go about completing them. The coordinator should also record his observations about the expectations of the student and his teacher on the second page of the research proposal, after the student has recorded his remarks. See Figure 6-B.

Independent Study Research Proposal

Pupil's Name: _____ _____
                          Last   First

_____

Student's statement of specific goals he wishes to achieve and how he plans to achieve them:

_____

Coordinator's comments and observations regarding the proposed research:

_____

Figure 6—B
Independent Study Research Proposal —Page 2

Before the student leaves, the coordinator should explain to the youngster the importance of the student summary sheets, Figure 6-C. These must be completed by the student on a regular basis and turned in

Independent Study Summary Sheet

Date: _____

Progress made:

Problems encountered:

Resources used:

_____

Date: _____

Progress made:

Problems encountered:

Resources used:

_____

Date: _____

Progress made:

Problems encountered:

Resources used:

_____

Figure 6–C
Student Summary Sheet for Independent Study

to the coordinator to keep him apprised of how the youngster is progressing in his research. Considering the age levels of middle school students and their lack of experience in the area of formal independent study, the coordinator should undoubtedly require many students to initially complete these brief forms on a daily basis. Others may have to turn them in every two or three days.

When the student has completed a section of the summary sheet he should place it in a designated in-basket in the coordinator's office. That evening the coordinator should review all of the sheets turned in by different students engaged in independent study projects, write pertinent comments on the sheets, and make note of those students he must see the next day to clarify certain points. The students should pick up their summary sheets the next morning in their own labeled mailboxes in the coordinator's office. This would give each student 24-hour feedback service on his project.

If the coordinator feels that one of the students is having a problem in an area in which he, the coordinator, lacks expertise, he should refer the pupil to one of the other staff members who is a specialist in that area. In an ungraded middle school as described in this book, personnel are always available in team planning rooms or in learning centers for consultation.

Evaluating Student Research

Since carefully planned independent study research projects can be of tremendous benefit to middle school students and their teachers, great care must be taken in evaluating these studies. For this reason the student, his teacher, and the Coordinator of Independent Study and Student Research should all play an active role in this evaluation.

Once the student's research has been completed and he has prepared his written report, it is recommended that the following procedures be followed:

1. The student, his teacher, and the coordinator should each read the report separately.

2. A conference should be scheduled at which time the student explains his research in detail to the teacher and the coordinator, who in turn have an opportunity to ask questions.

3. Each is asked to evaluate the study in terms of a five-point rating scale: excellent, good, average, below average, and poor. Each makes his determination without consulting with the other two. Their judgments are recorded on the form provided, Figure 6-D.

Independent Study Evaluation Sheet

Pupil's Name: _____ _____ Date: _____
                        Last   First

Rating Scale: Excellent, good, average, below average, or poor.

Student's evaluation: _____ Teacher's evaluation: _____

Coordinator's evaluation: _____ Others involved: _____

                                      Final evaluation: _____

Teacher's comments:

Coordinator's comments:

Figure 6–D
Independent Study Evaluation Sheet

4. While the teacher and the coordinator are completing their evaluations and making pertinent written comments concerning the study and its defense, the student is asked to complete a more detailed evaluation of his own research and of the program itself. See Figure 6-E.

5. The student, the teacher, and the coordinator discuss their analysis of the study and attempt to arrive at a mutually agreed upon final overall evaluation.

6. Four copies of the final evaluation are prepared. One is placed in the student's permanent file, a second is mailed with an accompanying letter to his parents or guardian, a third copy is given to the student, and the fourth is kept by the coordinator.

The dialogue that takes place among the student, his teacher, and the coordinator demands that the youngster have a thorough understanding of

Student Self-Evaluation

Pupil's Name:_____ _____ Date: _____
　　　　　　　　　Last　　　　　First

---

1. Why did you evaluate your research as you did?

2. Were you satisfied with the operations of the independent study program?

3. What specific advantages did you feel this research offered you?

4. What specific problems did you encounter?

5. Do you have any recommendations or suggestions to make con- concerning the independent study program?

6. Do you plan on pursuing independent study programs in the future?

Additional student comments:

Figure 6—E
Independent Study Student Self-Evaluation

his study and that his teacher and the coordinator be familiar with it in order to ask probing questions. This conference can help the student to gain new insight into the educational process. As he discusses his research the student is required to think on his feet, develop concise logical explanations to clarify vague areas in his research, and defend his point of view. He hopefully will view the coordinator and his teacher as consultants and helpful inquirers in the undertaking, and no longer as mere dispensers of information or harsh and unfair critics. The one-to-one relationships developed during the course of the research study are at the core of the program and should influence the future behavior of both the student and his teacher. The atmosphere in which these oral defenses are conducted should be far superior to the traditional paper and pencil evaluation techniques.

Having read the report and thoroughly examined the student's research in the conference, the coordinator, the teacher, and the pupil should be well prepared to evaluate the project in terms of the goals and criteria agreed to at the beginning of the study. No letter or numerical grade should be written on the report or included in the evaluation process. Since the student had pursued an area of interest to him, and was not just seeking a numerical or alphabetical reward, the evaluation should be in general terms that focus on the study itself, both in its written form and its oral defense.

In addition to this the student, in completing his self-evaluation sheet, will give the coordinator and his teacher further insight into how the independent study program is functioning. From suggestions made and comments noted, steps can be taken to improve the program. This will also require the youngster to analyze once again how he functioned working on his own.

Once the student, his teacher, the coordinator, and any other parties involved in the project have completed their evaluations, they should discuss the rationale underlying their judgments. Since the independent study program involves cooperation from many quarters, it is only logical that the final evaluation be the result of such a discussion and an averaging of the three or more views of the study. All parties must share equally in this process. Usually there is a very high correlation among the evaluators because all have been working together and have come to know and respect each other's judgment.

Since grades are still required in most schools, and since students willingly involve themselves in independent study projects in lieu of attending a regularly scheduled class, different methods can be used to determine the influence of the independent study research project on the report card grade in the subject matter area in which the research was conducted.

1. The student's report card grade can be determined just by using the marks he received when he was present in the class. While this would exclude the independent study from the average, indication could be made on the card that such a study has been completed.

2. The pupil's average can be determined by combining marks received in class with the final overall evaluation of the independent study

project. This means that the latter rating would have to be converted to a numerical grade and then averaged in with the other marks.

The second alternative seems to be the more realistic one and is recommended by this author.

Total Effectiveness of the Program

Once the independent study program has been launched and a coordinator employed on a full-time basis, it is essential that the entire operation be thoroughly analyzed at the conclusion of each school year. The following criteria should be used to arrive at valid judgments concerning the overall effectiveness of the independent study program:

1. *The number of students participating in the program.* While the number of pupils initially undertaking studies may be small, if at least 20 percent of the student population becomes involved in the program during its first year of operation, the program should be considered successful. After the second year, better than 40 percent must be involved at one time or another for the program to be considered a success.

2. *The number of teachers involved in the program.* If the number of teachers allowing students to pursue independent study programs is continually on the increase, then the program can be considered success-ful. Within the first five months at least 25 percent of the staff should have been involved in the program. At the conclusion of the first year at least half of the staff should have had at least one of their students involved in an independent study research project for the program to be considered a success.

3. *The number of teams involved in the program.* If students from every team in the building are involved in the independent study program at one time or another throughout the year, the program can be considered successful. Careful analysis will reveal those teams that are not taking advantage of the situation. Appropriate steps will have to be taken with these teams.

4. *The willingness of students to engage in future independent study research projects after completing their first undertaking.* If better than 50 percent of the students involved in independent study undertake a second study during the course of the year, the program is considered to be successful. If 90 percent of those who were involved in independent study indicate on their self-evaluation sheets that they liked the program and are desirous of pursuing more independent study projects in the future, the program can also be considered a success.

5. *An analysis of the independent evaluations of the students, their teachers, and the coordinator.* If there is a considerable degree of

consensus among the evaluators regarding the research, the program is to be considered successful.

6. *The comments of teachers whose students pursue independent study projects.* If the vast majority of teachers whose students have been involved in independent study projects comment favorably on the program, it can be viewed as being successful.

If at least five of these six criteria are fulfilled, the independent study program can be judged to be a total success. If four of six are fulfilled, the program is satisfactory but improvement is needed. If less than four are met, there should be a thorough analysis of the entire program to determine modifications necessary for its continuance.

Summary

If the ungraded middle school is to achieve two of its primary goals, namely the individualization of instruction and the development of those qualities that will make students independent learners, it must provide opportunities for students to pursue independent study research projects in areas of interest to them in lieu of attending certain classes. These student-initiated studies must be carried on within a structure that will insure the success of the research. Thus there is a need for a Coordinator of Independent Study and Student Research to see that once the student has met the criteria required for participation in the program the operation will run smoothly and efficiently.

It is essential for the coordinator to sell himself and his program to teachers and students for it to succeed. By having the entire independent study program well organized with appropriate forms and procedures to be followed, as well as employing various techniques for evaluating both student projects and the program itself, students and staff will have confidence in the program and its coordinator. This should result in more middle school students demonstrating an ability to think analytically and critically, understand basic techniques of research, separate fact from opinion before reaching decisions, make deductions and inferences, and summarize and defend their findings concisely and logically in their own words.

When an independent study program helps the student to develop self-confidence, responsibility, a critical, questioning attitude, an ability to make crucial decisions, to be selective, and enables him to acquire the skills essential to the pursuit of his goals, the program is then a vital part of the ungraded middle school.

Chapter 7

The Middle School Principalship

MAJOR IMPROVEMENTS IN the quality of educational programs for early adolescents will only be achieved when basic changes are made in previously existing organizational and instructional practices. The building principal, because of the considerable authority that is attached to his position, can either serve as an impetus or a hindrance for these much needed changes.

This chapter will focus on the qualities that the middle school principal must possess to be successful, along with an examination of his overall duties and responsibilities. The necessity for sharing his decision-making powers with the other members of the building leadership team as well as with the various teaching teams will be explored. Budgetary procedures consistent with the school's educational goals and plans to make maximum use of existing physical facilities will be analyzed. Techniques to be employed in evaluating teacher and team performances, along with methods for keeping all apprised of the instructional programs in progress, will be studied. Finally, the principal's role in disciplinary matters will be examined and his relationships with students, staff, central office personnel, and the community will be scrutinized.

Essential Qualities for a Middle School Principal

To be successful the principal of an ungraded middle school must:

1. Demonstrate to teachers, students, parents, and central office

personnel that he possesses a thorough understanding of all aspects of the operations of an ungraded middle school.

2. Clarify his role in the school and the expectations that he has for staff.

3. Inspire and excite his teachers to meet the challenges presented by their new working conditions.

4. Encourage teachers and other members of the building leadership team to be innovative.

5. Show discriminating insight and understanding in the deployment of personnel so that the personal aspirations of staff members are achieved along with the educational goals of the school.

6. Share certain decision-making responsibilities with teachers and students.

7. Work cooperatively with the entire staff in developing outstanding curricular programs and instructional practices.

8. Provide facilities and circumstances that will release the abilities and potentialities of teachers and students.

9. Evaluate all personnel in a manner that will have beneficial effects on the school.

10. Make decisions that are consistent with the school's educational philosophy, regardless of pressures brought to bear on him.

As plans are being formulated in a district for the transition from a junior high school to an ungraded middle school, the principal's depth of knowledge about the entire program will be severely tested. He must not only be able to point out, clearly and dispassionately, to parents and teachers, the rationale for the move and how it will benefit the students and staff but must also seek opportunities to do so. Examples must be cited and research must be unearthed to support his position. If the principal, when asked specific questions regarding nongradedness, independent study, reporting pupil progress, and interdisciplinary team teaching, responds immediately with concrete examples to illustrate different points, people will respect his intelligence and his judgment. Evasive answers will immediately place the entire undertaking in jeopardy.

The overall plans for the operations of the middle school and the well organized manner in which they are developed, explained, and refined will do much to convince staff of the merits of the move. If the teachers are truly convinced, they will convey a positive image of the project to their students and to the community.

In this author's professional opinion if the ungraded middle school is to succeed, the building principal must serve as a coordinator and a supporter, helping teachers and teams to implement the program. His role must be other than an authoritarian one, except when necessary. It is extremely important that the principal convey this message to the teachers. His actions over a period of time will demonstrate to them whether or not he is in concert with his previously announced role and will influence their activities accordingly.

Aside from explaining his functions as he views them and perhaps modifying them with suggestions from staff as to how they would like him to function, it is essential that the building principal indicate what he initially expects of his staff. It is extremely important in the hiring of new teachers that they be aware of what is expected of them in the areas of interdisciplinary teamwork, grouping practices, and the use of independent study. The principal's initial expectations of staff should be realistic but challenging. He should state that he hopes to have each member of the staff attempting to develop appropriate individualized instructional programs for their students by means of a team approach. Teachers will then realize that the building principal expects them to perform in accordance with the previously established goals of the ungraded middle school. This is a most reasonable request to make when the program begins since an Instructional Consultant, a Coordinator of Independent Study and Student Research, guidance counselors and central office personnel, in addition to the principal, will be available to help them.

The building principal must himself be enthusiastic about the program to be launched in the middle school if he expects staff to become excited about the undertaking. He must be firmly convinced that an ungraded middle school organized on an interdisciplinary team basis, with opportunities for interested students to pursue independent study, can achieve goals only dreamed of in the past, and thus his enthusiasm should rub off on those with whom he comes in contact. Ideally an innovative principal should possess the ability to make his teachers believe in him and his ideas. Staff must be convinced that he can "bring the whole thing off" with their cooperation. This calls for a principal of unusual leadership ability. The insecure, plodding, humdrum type of administrator, which unfortunately abounds in secondary schools, cannot be successful in this type of situation.

Since the principal's educational and operational philosophy places much greater faith and responsibility in the collective abilities of teachers than in the past, it is easy for many staff members to become excited about their new working conditions. Many teachers are eager to exercise both their personal and professional judgments and see their recommendations directly affect the operation of the school. Teachers in the ungraded middle school will be challenged to act as professionals, making diagnoses of student needs, prescribing specific instructional programs, and evaluating the results of their work. The possibility of new relationships with colleagues, students, and administrators, while frightening to some, will serve to attract teacher candidates to the school and excite those deciding to remain on the staff.

The principal can best demonstrate support for his staff and the encouragement of innovative ideas by the manner in which he operates when ideas or suggestions are made to him and by the freedom he gives his teachers. He must be an encourager, never a discourager, and be continuously open to suggestions. But without appearing to be placing educational roadblocks in the path of new ideas, the building principal must always require a sound rationale from the teacher for an idea before endorsing the request.

The principal's decision to have an Instructional Consultant rather than an assistant principal is a clear example of the support he is willing to give his teachers. The latitude which the building principal gives the I. C. as well as the Coordinator of Independent Study and Student Research is another indication of his support for new ideas.

The deployment of teachers and the manner in which interdisciplinary teams are formed will have great bearing on the success of the middle school. While it has previously been stated that teachers must play an active role in interviewing teacher candidates and making recommendations as to the personnel composing different interdisciplinary teams, the building principal still retains the final decision-making responsibility. He must integrate his own perceptions of how teachers should be deployed with the opinions expressed by members of the professional staff. To make the correct decisions he must know his teachers and be able to predict how they will act and react if and when they are teamed with different individuals. Various combinations of teachers as teams must be discussed and analyzed on the planning board by the leadership team.

Since a "staffing pattern is a concrete manifestation of philosophical positions regarding the nature of knowledge, the nature of learning and teaching, and the nature of man,"[1] it is vital that the principal be conscious of each staff member's views in these areas. The principal must be able to select and bring together teachers of widely varying talents and backgrounds and get them to work as cohesive units. To accomplish this he should be aware of research findings relating to teamwork dispositions in different individuals. For example Perez has found that "chronological age is a critical factor for manifestation of teamwork and authoritarianism in teacher personality. Young women and old men teachers are disposed

---

1. Fenwick English, "Teacher May I? Take Three Giant Steps! The Differentiated Staff," *Phi Delta Kappan,* Vol. 51, No. 4, December, 1969, p. 211.

toward teamwork while young men and old women teachers incline toward authoritarianism."[2] He further stated that

> The disposition toward authoritarianism and teamwork in a male and female teacher changes with the acquisition of experience. Apparently, forces are at work to alter type of reaction effected to educational stimuli as the individual matures with the teaching assignment. This works inversely with the two sexes. Thus, a man will move from high disposition toward authoritarianism to a low disposition toward authoritarianism and from a low degree of teamwork disposition to a high degree of teamwork disposition. A woman will move from a low disposition toward authoritarianism to a high disposition toward authoritarianism and from a high degree of teamwork disposition to a low degree of teamwork disposition.[3]

These vital pieces of information, combined with his own perceptions and those of others whose opinions he respects, should provide the building principal with enough data to make the best possible use of his staff. If this is not done and teachers are poorly deployed, dissatisfaction will result and teacher morale in the school will be low, with a resulting loss in program effectiveness.

With all that is going on in the new ungraded middle school, and with more and more being expected of teaching and administrative personnel, it is essential that the building principal delegate certain decision-making prerogatives to teachers and students if the goals of the school are to be achieved. Evidence

> indicates that teachers who actively participate in the decision-making process exhibit greater job satisfaction than do those to whom such opportunity has been denied. The obvious implication for the principal's behavior is that he should involve his teachers in making decisions which affect them.[4]

The teachers and the teaching teams must therefore be given the freedom to make those decisions that directly affect their:

1. Assignment to teams;
2. Students' schedules;
3. Grouping of students;
4. Use of instructional and noninstructional time; and
5. Development of appropriate curricular programs for their students.

---

2. Joseph Francis Perez, *A Study to Determine the Relationship Between the Position of Teachers on the California F. Scale and Their Disposition Toward Teamwork* (Doctoral Dissertation; The University of Connecticut, 1959), pp. 84-85.

3. *Ibid.*, p. 96.

4. Samuel Goldman, *The School Principal* (New York: The Center For Applied Research in Education, Inc., 1966), p. 60.

This demands the creation of a master schedule that will give responsibility to the teachers and their students for the appropriate use of time and facilities to accomplish specific tasks. Just as teachers must feel free to excuse certain pupils from regularly scheduled classes to pursue independent study projects, students must also feel free to initiate such requests and to assume some responsibility for the conduct of their peer group in such areas of the building as the student commons and the learning centers. By delegating such responsibilities, the building principal can help students to become independent learners and can enable teachers to function as professional educators.

The principal, by the manner in which he allows the Instructional Consultant to operate, as described in chapter 5, will do much to encourage the development of outstanding curricular programs and instructional practices. He himself, by his presence at team planning sessions, by his frequent classroom visitations, by his overall attitude towards programs already in progress and others on the planning board, and by the credit he gives others for jobs well done, can create a climate that encourages experimentation and active teacher participation in curriculum matters.

The building principal must exercise patience in waiting to see positive results from the new structure. In the interim he must continually work with and educate his teachers to the fact that many existing educational practices

> fail to provide students with opportunities to experience what is involved in decision making and choice, the establishment of meaning, the use of evidence and logic, and collaboration toward proximate goals. Instead, they afford narrow, formalized introductions to a string of disconnected subjects, superficially considered through emphasis upon nomenclature, classification systems, or the manipulation of paraphernalia. Separation of information and the problems and issues to which it applies unfortunately still characterizes segments of American . . . education.[5]

Once having described the educational scene in such terms, he must convince the staff of his faith in them and their ability to change this pattern, thus making the students' education vibrant, transitional, and dynamic.

The only way for the principal to provide his staff with the best possible facilities and circumstances in which to work is to develop a master schedule that maximizes the full potential of the existing physical facilities. Later in this chapter examples will be presented demonstrating

---

5. George W. Denemark, "Teacher Education: Repair, Reform, or Revolution?" *Educational Leadership,* Vol. 27, No. 6, March, 1970, pp. 539-540.

how creative use of physical facilities can enable program goals to be achieved. The manner in which the master schedule deploys teacher and student time will determine to a large extent whether or not the school's objectives are reached.

For years teachers have complained, with justification, that they have not been able to do what was necessary for their students because of a rigid, inflexible master schedule. Therefore it is extremely important that a schedule be developed that is flexible enough to give teachers and students opportunities to display their creative talents. It must be remembered that

> One of the most important functions a principal fulfills is constructing the school schedule. As he does this, he orders a student's day, he deploys a teacher's talent, and he establishes the climate for learning. The school schedule establishes the means by which its instructional ends can be adequately achieved.
>
> Only a principal who knows his staff and who has a clear idea about the purposes of a secondary school can hope to be a positive force in the school. The school schedule is the evidence of this knowledge. The master schedule is the vehicle for activating what the princpal believes about student needs and teacher capabilities.[6]

As the principal visits classrooms and attends team planning sessions, he is making judgments about individual teacher performances. While these formal and informal evaluations are being made, it is important that they be shared openly and honestly with the personnel involved. Too often in the past accurate evaluations of an individual's performance have either not been made or not been conveyed to the staff member. This has caused many teachers to be concerned, for they are not aware of how they are viewed by their building administrator. Each teacher has a right to be evaluated and to be informed of the evaluator's reaction to his performance as this has a direct bearing not only on the teacher's employment-tenure status, but also on his performance level. A teacher who is evaluated infrequently will soon come to view the entire procedure, when and if it is conducted, with disdain, or at best, with disinterest.

Principals must therefore regularly evaluate teachers and other personnel in terms of their effectiveness in achieving the educational objectives to which the school is committed. This means that in the nongraded middle school, teachers will have to be evaluated both as individuals and as members of teams. While always seeking to make the

---

6. From *Flexible Scheduling: Bold New Venture,* by Donald C. Manlove & David W. Beggs, III. Copyright © 1965 by Indiana University Press. Reprinted by permission of the publisher, p. 33.

process a positive one, and employing such techniques as pre-observation and post-observation conferences before and after all formal classroom visits, the principal must not shirk from playing the heavy when it appears that an individual, tenured or non-tenured, is performing unsatisfactorily and not showing improvement. While conveying his professional evaluation of the situation to the teacher, both verbally and in writing, the building principal can seek to use a variety of resources, including the I. C. and fellow teachers, to help the individual experiencing difficulty. In justice to the students however, and in the best interests of the school, if a teacher is not working out, he must be removed from his position.

Regardless of how good the total orientation has been, there is bound to be some criticism of the school's innovations. The principal must remain cool in the face of such challenges, answer his critics calmly, with evidence to refute their contentions, admit when and where mistakes have been made, and indicate the corrective steps that are planned to resolve the problems encountered. He must continually support his staff in their attempts to individualize instructional programs.

His steadiness, confident spirit, and his continual adherence to the philosophical and operational principles on which the school is based will indicate to staff his total commitment to the program. This will help teachers to function more effectively since they will realize that they have the complete support of their educational leader.

Additional Duties and Responsibilities

In addition to the tasks described in the preceding section, the middle school building principal may also be responsible to the superintendent of schools to:

1. Develop a program of extra-curricular activities and supervise the handling of all funds and accounts involved.

2. Compile data for reports as are required for attendance, report card, and payroll purposes.

3. Supervise the activities of the various non-teaching personnel assigned to the building.

4. Submit an annual budget.

5. Approve the use of school facilities by outside organizations, keeping within the bounds of board of education policy.

6. Distribute all textbooks, supplies, and equipment requisitioned.

7. Check on the sanitation and safety of the buildings and grounds and see that all state and local regulations are complied with.

8. Cooperate with parent and other lay groups interested in promoting the educational welfare of children.

9. Approve all purchase requisitions and verify accounts for payment.

10. Set up a system of compiling a school newsletter which may be used for public relations purposes.

11. Work cooperatively with central office personnel including directors, coordinators, and consultants, in the furtherance of district programs.

It is imperative that the principal delegate some of the tasks which are really non-instructional in nature to other personnel, such as an efficient secretary. Then he can have more time to work with teachers and students to improve the educational programs offered in the school.

Sharing Decision-Making Powers

The middle school cannot achieve one of its primary goals, namely that of helping early adolescents become independent learners, if staff is not permitted to make both independent and collective judgments about what students need in the line of instructional programs. This demands that members of the leadership team as well as teachers on both interdisciplinary and related arts teams be given the opportunity to make those decisions that directly affect them and those with whom they work. This is a logical, operational extension of the middle school philosophy.

The delegation of authority to others greatly enhances the possibility for creative innovations since many minds can often be more fruitful than one. But there is also an inherent risk in giving freedom and responsibility to others. Some mistakes are bound to be made in this new endeavor. If a few errors are not made, it generally indicates that the staff is not really trying to innovate. But the principal must have the courage to take these risks for it is impossible to have an ungraded middle school operating on an interdisciplinary basis without giving the teams the authority they require to function effectively. The mistakes however can be kept to a minimum by the quality of the in-service educational program conducted by qualified personnel prior to the opening of the school.

While not abrogating in any sense of the word his responsibility for the total operations of the building, the principal must delegate various responsibilities to appropriate personnel capable of handling them. This should enable him to get staff more involved, and thus more committed, to the program. This will allow leadership to emerge from various parts of the building at different times as occasions warrant. Advocates of this type of organized permissiveness see each type of team as a

federation of equals, with each member assuming responsibility for those functions for which he is the most qualified person on the team. Proponents of this model claim that morale is higher and individual involvement is greater when the contributions of each member receive equal reward and recognition. It is claimed that the "emerging leadership" pattern is more consistent with the actual situation in most schools, with different teachers possessing special competencies in different areas.[7]

Thus the principal must allow the other three members of his building leadership team, the Instructional Consultant, the Coordinator of Independent Study and Student Research, and the Pupil Personnel Consultant, to have autonomy in operating within their respective areas. He however must still accept responsibility for their activities. This requires that the principal be a secure individual, willing to let others take responsibility in certain areas, but always ready to publicly stand the brunt of criticism for errors that are made and problems that develop. While the building principal may "chew out" the individual in charge of a specific area in private for a serious blunder, in public he must take full responsibility for the error, assuring all parties concerned that corrective steps will be taken at once.

The Pupil Personnel Consultant, the Instructional Consultant, and the Coordinator of Independent Study and Student Research, must be expected to work in concert with the principal and with the teams in achieving the school's goals. Continual failure of any one of them to operate in a manner consistent with the school's educational philosophy should result in the dismissal of that individual. But the principal must truly give each the responsibility for the area assigned to him if he is to hold them accountable to him for their area.

This means that the principal must let the Coordinator handle the entire independent study program. It is "his baby." Its successes are his successes. Its failures however will unfortunately be the building principal's. This is the reality of the situation and why the building principal is paid the salary he receives. The same philosophy applies to the I. C. for the instructional program and to the Pupil Personnel Consultant for the guidance program.

Just as the principal must give the leadership team members responsibilities and the support of his office, the same philosophy must prevail in his dealings with teachers and teams. To refuse to grant this is to doom the middle school undertaking to failure. It is an established fact that class size should be determined by what is to be taught, to whom, and for what purposes. The individuals in the best position to make such judgments are the teachers of the students involved, not the administrator. The teachers are also in the best position to judge how long it will take to develop the

---

7. William M. Alexander and others, *The Emergent Middle School,* Second, Enlarged Edition (New York: Holt, Rinehart and Winston, Inc., 1968), p. 109.

lesson on a particular day, when during the day it should be taught, and what instructional techniques need to be employed with different groups.

Therefore teachers must make decisions regarding the use of their time as well as that of their students and determine how their students are to be grouped and scheduled if the goals of the schools are to be attained. This requires that the building principal establish a framework which will give them the freedom they require. Figures 4-J, 4-K, and 4-L have already shown how this can be done by employing block-time scheduling.

If the principal should be foolish enough to be authoritarian in his ways while at the same time attempting to implement some of the innovations described throughout this book, his staff will become more and more dependent on him for specific, detailed directions. If projects fail and problems occur, teachers can correctly say that it isn't their fault, for they only did what the principal told them to do. This is certainly not in keeping with the operational philosophy of the ungraded middle school.

Personnel must realize that it is not an easy thing for many administrators to delegate responsibility. But the delegation of authority is an absolute necessity for the successful operation of the ungraded middle school. Ingils has pointed out the trauma that some administrators experience when required to do this. He explains this as follows:

> Because of the competitive environment in which he has worked and progressed through the ranks, he often is concerned about the competition he will experience from subordinates. A latent fear of this competition causes him to be afraid that his subordinates will do the work as well as he can—or maybe better.[8]

If the building principal refuses to delegate authority no matter what the reason is, he is handicapping the school's progress. At this point the superintendent of schools or his aides, especially the assistant superintendent for instruction or the director of secondary education, must work with the building principal to correct the situation or else recommend to the board of education that he be removed from a leadership role he can no longer fulfill.

If students are to be expected to become independent learners, they must be given opportunities to demonstrate that they can handle various types of responsibilities, both at home and in school. By allowing students to play a more active role in the operations of the school, by establishing a structure within which they can pursue research without the direct supervision of others, by permitting them to move through the building

---

8. Chester Ingils, "Advice to Administrators: Clues for Success," *The Clearing House*, Vol. 42, No. 1, September 1967, p. 15.

without passes from their teachers, and by providing them with a student commons relaxation center for which they are responsible, the principal is demonstrating his faith in the student. Giving pupils opportunities to elect some of the subjects they wish to take is another way the principal can delegate some of his responsibility. Areas such as these can certainly be handled well by young adolescents if their teachers, counselors, and administrators are willing to work cooperatively with them.

Budgetary Procedures

An ungraded middle school must adopt budgetary procedures far different from most prevailing methods of budget development. In too many school districts a building budget is developed by taking the number of students to be enrolled in the school and multiplying that figure by a cost factor. This cost factor is usually derived from analyzing the district's previous spending records. Thus the total cost per pupil, exclusive of the salaries of paid employees, debt service, and transportation, is multiplied by the number of pupils in the school, and a figure is arrived at which in essence becomes the school's operating budget for the year. Nowhere in these calculations or in these procedures is consideration given to the instructional program and what it requires.

A building budget must be a financial statement of the school's instructional program, nothing more and nothing less than that. Many districts still have one cost factor of spending for an elementary school pupil, and a slightly higher one for a secondary school pupil, and these two figures alone are used to develop the school's basic budget. Some districts even impose more restrictions on the development of the budget, establishing expenditures per child in the areas of textbooks, general classroom supplies, and special area supplies for art, music, industrial arts, and home economics. Again little if any mention is made of the financial needs of the instructional program.

Once the central office personnel have developed these figures they are either given to the building principal with the direction that he is to operate within the total dollar figure indicated or else the figure is withheld until the principal and his staff have spent many hours developing a realistic budget at which point they are informed that since their requests are too high, they must cut their budget to the predetermined figure established by the central office. The latter approach is very frustrating to the principal and his staff who immediately feel that they have been taken advantage of. The budgetary process then disintegrates into a type of negotiations between the building principal and his staff on the one hand and the district office on the other. The principal and his teachers pad the budget knowing it will be cut. The district office presents its unrealistically low figures and some type of compromise evolves. This type of unprofessional game is not in the best interests of either the students or the taxpayers of the community.

To enable the ungraded middle school to achieve its goals, it is recommended that the following procedures be employed in developing a budget:

1. The building principal should meet with the entire staff to explain the procedures to be followed in developing the budget. At that time he must make it clear to all that the budget must be a financial representation of the school's educational program. Therefore padding will not be allowed.

2. The principal, within one week after this initial meeting, should schedule meetings with each of the interdisciplinary teams as well as with the related arts teams to further clarify the entire process and to answer any questions. The Instructional Consultant should also be present at these sessions to make appropriate comments regarding the educational programs and instructional practices currently in effect and others planned for in the future.

3. The budget must be prepared by teaching teams, not by departments. Traditionally all the English teachers met and developed a budget for their department. The same situation prevailed in other subject matter areas. There is no room for such an approach in the ungraded middle school. Instead budgets must be submitted by each of the school's teaching teams as well as by the building leadership team. This is the key to the entire budgetary process. The teachers on a team know their students and what they need. Since each team will be having many of the same students again the following year, it is in the best possible position to develop the budget it needs.

4. An item-by-item justification budget must be developed by each team in the building. This means that, aside from general supply items such as paper, stencils, chalk, etc., which are ordered automatically by the principal or his secretary, all other budgetary requests need to be justified in terms of the educational programs to be offered the following year. To order any item costing over 75 dollars per unit price, the teacher or the team must develop a short, concise, well written paragraph stating why the item is needed. Convenient forms should be prepared by the principal's office to facilitate this operation.

5. One month after the meetings with each of the teams, the budgets should be turned in to the principal. After the principal and the I. C. have reviewed them carefully and noted areas of concern, a meeting should be scheduled with each team to finalize its budget. Thus any fat

will be cut out of the budget before it leaves the building to go to the central office. If a teacher or a team can't logically explain and defend an item in their budget, the item is removed. Such an internal professional analysis of the budget by the principal, the I. C., and the teams results in a neat, compact budget that can easily be explained and defended if necessary. This of course means that since different teams have different students with different needs, each team's budget will differ.

6. After this meeting each team should have two weeks to review its budget, make alterations, and return it to the principal for final analysis.

7. In reviewing the team's budgets, the quality and the quantity of the items recommended for purchase must reflect the needs of the students, not just teacher preferences, and must conform to the school's educational philosophy. For example, an ungraded middle school organized on an interdisciplinary team basis cannot have any of its teams ordering one hundred copies of a certain textbook if it truly subscribes to an individualized approach but also a multi-media approach since students learn in a variety of ways. As teachers and teams are encouraged and given active support to develop appropriate curricular programs, more ditto paper and stencils will be used, more transparencies will be developed, more paperbacks will be consumed and fewer textbooks and encyclopedias will be ordered. There will be and should be a shift from previous budgetary priorities.

It must also be understood that not every student needs a textbook for each subject, nor do all students need the same text for the same subject. This is difficult for some parents and teachers to comprehend. The term "multitext" has also led to a good deal of confusion. Some think that it means that each student has several textbooks for the same subject. Such is not generally the case although at times and for definite reasons it may be. The multitext approach simply means that the school is no longer ordering large numbers of a single textbook to be used with all students in a particular subject matter area. It does imply that teachers are being directed to carefully examine the materials currently on the market, matching them to the divergent needs and learning styles of their students, and ordering accordingly.

8. The principal, his secretary, and the Instructional Consultant, after receiving the budgets from all of the teams, should compile the school's total budget by combining the items requested by the various teams with the standard list of general supply-consumable items the school needs. The later figure can be arrived at from an experience factor. The total package reflecting each team's budget, with written statements explaining the rationale for specific items plus the general, annual needs of

the school, and covering letters from both the building principal and the Instructional Consultant, should then be forwarded to the designated person in the district office.

9. Within one month after the budget has been sent to the district office for review, the principal and the I. C. should meet with the assistant superintendent for instructional services, the assistant superintendent for business, and the director of secondary education, and the superintendent of schools if he is available, to explain and defend the budget and the educational program it represents. At this meeting the school's educational leaders should clarify all areas of concern, indicating that they did cutting in their own building prior to sending the budget to the district office. If for certain reasons the superintendent declares that the total budget for the school, although a good one and a realistic one, must be cut, the principal should go back to his staff, inform them of the situation, and request their help in reducing the budget. This can best be done by having each team establish priorities within their budgets, getting all the teams together, and cooperatively deciding what must be cut first to reach the figure requested by the superintendent. But in no case must the building principal allow central office personnel to cut his budget for him.

10. A certain amount of money must also be allocated by the principal and the Instructional Consultant for unexpected situations that may arise during the course of the year.

If these procedures are followed the students, teachers, and taxpayers should get top educational value for their dollar.

Maximum Use of Physical Facilities

Schools must no longer be organized simply for administrative convenience, but must operate in ways that facilitate the attainment of the school's instructional objectives. This is especially true with regard to the use of existing physical facilities. Many teachers and administrators incorrectly contend that the programs described throughout this book cannot be implemented in their traditionally designed buildings. They erroneously state that the ungraded middle school can't begin to function effectively unless it has both open space areas and a large learning resource center. While these open spaced facilities are desirable, they are not essential to the launching of an ungraded middle school organized on an interdisciplinary teaming basis.

Figures 7-A through 7-D illustrate various plant designs that have been used by building principals to house creative middle school programs. Two of these physical facilities are designed around the open space concept while the other two are more typical of school structures found in most communities. Each plant however has the potential to house an exciting educational program. Therefore it must be clearly understood that it is mental rather than physical barriers that prevent the launching of new programs. If an administrator and his staff want to achieve specific educational and instructional goals, they can and will find ways to accomplish this within the existing facilities. On the other hand, no matter how modern and up-to-date the physical facilities are, if teachers and administrators are not committed to a new program, it will not become operational. Thus good design can enhance the program but poor design cannot prevent it from functioning.

Figures 7-A and 7-B depict middle schools that depart radically in their construction from traditionally designed buildings for young adolescents. For example, the Big Walnut Middle School, Sunbury, Ohio, see Figure 7-A, is a 600 pupil plant that features:

A. Three learning centers which are the equivalent of seven standard-sized classrooms;
B. Carpeting and air conditioning in the academic areas;
C. A 3500 sq. ft. library facility that includes an area set aside for teacher planning; and
D. No permanent inside walls.

This school was specifically designed to implement a team teaching approach to instruction.

Figure 7-B is the proposed scheme for a middle school in Howard County, Maryland which also exemplifies the open space concept designed specifically to implement a flexible middle school program. Figure 7-C illustrates how the Jamesville-Dewitt Middle School, Jamesville, New York, is divided up into three distinct houses, each having sixth, seventh, and eighth grade students, and the staff employing an interdisciplinary instructional approach.

When the staff of the Liverpool Junior High School was faced with the task of launching an ungraded middle school program in a traditionally designed building, a hard look was taken at the existing physical plant. Priorities were established that were considered to be essential for putting the school's philosophy into practice. The priorities were:

A. Each team had to have a planning room.
B. Each team had to have a planning period every day when all members of the team would be free at the same time.
C. A room had to be set aside for the Coordinator of Independent Study and Student Research.
D. There had to be a faculty dining room.

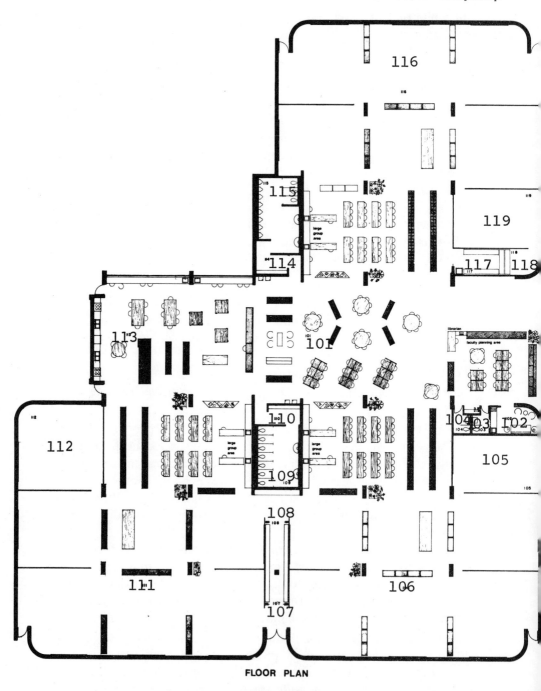

FLOOR PLAN

Figure 7-A
The Big Walnut Middle School
Courtesy of Mr. Hylen Souders, Superintendent, Sunbury, Ohio

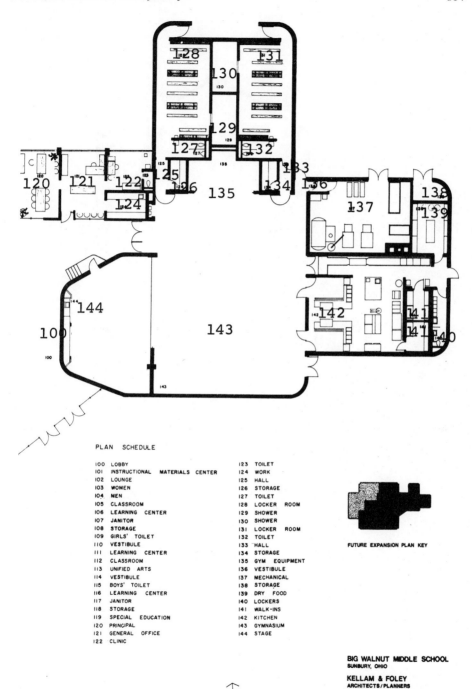

PLAN SCHEDULE

100	LOBBY	123	TOILET
101	INSTRUCTIONAL MATERIALS CENTER	124	WORK
102	LOUNGE	125	HALL
103	WOMEN	126	STORAGE
104	MEN	127	TOILET
105	CLASSROOM	128	LOCKER ROOM
106	LEARNING CENTER	129	SHOWER
107	JANITOR	130	SHOWER
108	STORAGE	131	LOCKER ROOM
109	GIRLS' TOILET	132	TOILET
110	VESTIBULE	133	HALL
111	LEARNING CENTER	134	STORAGE
112	CLASSROOM	135	GYM EQUIPMENT
113	UNIFIED ARTS	136	VESTIBULE
114	VESTIBULE	137	MECHANICAL
115	BOYS' TOILET	138	STORAGE
116	LEARNING CENTER	139	DRY FOOD
117	JANITOR	140	LOCKERS
118	STORAGE	141	WALK-INS
119	SPECIAL EDUCATION	142	KITCHEN
120	PRINCIPAL	143	GYMNASIUM
121	GENERAL OFFICE	144	STAGE
122	CLINIC		

FUTURE EXPANSION PLAN KEY

N

BIG WALNUT MIDDLE SCHOOL
SUNBURY, OHIO

KELLAM & FOLEY
ARCHITECTS/PLANNERS

COLUMBUS, OHIO
INDIANAPOLIS, INDIANA

Figure 7-A (continued)

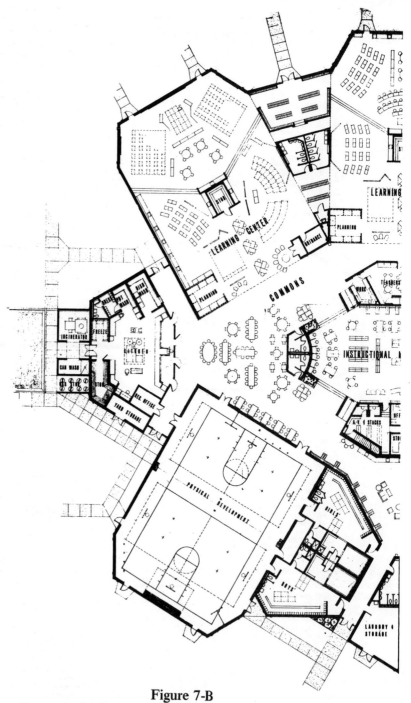

Figure 7-B
Proposed Scheme for a Howard County Middle School
Courtesy of Dr. John G. Freudenberger, Coordinator, Title III Program

Figure 7-B (continued)

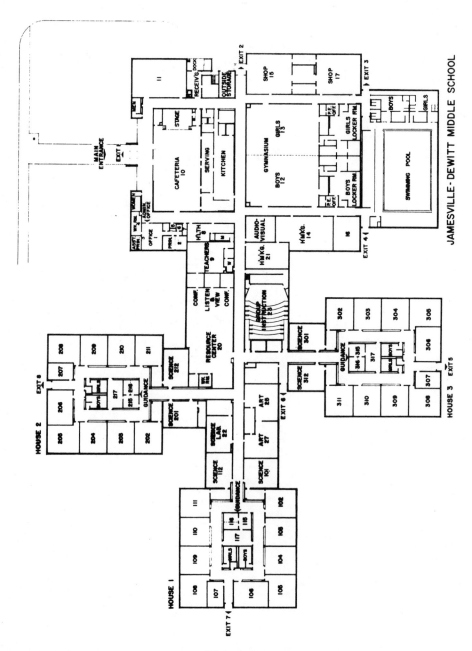

Figure 7-C
The Jamesville-Dewitt Middle School
Courtesy of Mr. Lansing Baker, Principal, Jamesville-Dewitt Middle School

E. At least two learning centers had to be established.

F. An area had to be set aside for a student commons relaxation center.

G. The teacher aides to be employed in the building had to have a work area.

H. Each team had to have a series of rooms provided for instructional purposes to be used by the team as it saw fit each day.

I. One large group instruction area had to be free each period of the day for use by teams.

As the teachers and the building leadership team analyzed the school facilities and how they had previously been deployed, Figures 7-D[1] and 7-D[2], it soon became apparent that by using a block-time schedule (see Figure 4-J), all the priorities could be met. Therefore the following changes were made in room usage in order to provide the basic physical facilities needed to launch the new program:

A. To set up a planning area for each interdisciplinary and related arts team, the following was done:

   1. Room 151, first floor, became a planning room for Team M.

   2. Room 110, first floor, became the planning room for Teams D and J. Each team's schedule was so arranged that they planned at different times, and the room was large enough for each teacher to have his own desk, chair, file cabinet, and bookcase.

   3. Room 411, first floor, became the planning room for Team L.

   4. Room 108, first floor, became the planning room for Teams I and H. The arrangement here was similar to room 110.

   5. The related arts team planned in room 104.

B. The planning periods established for each team were as follows:

   Team M, 2:05- 2:50 P.M.
   Team I, 1:15- 2:00 P.M.
   Team D, 1:15- 2:00 P.M.
   Team L, 8:45- 9:27 A.M.
   Team J, 9:30-10:12 A.M.
   Team H, 8:45- 9:27 A.M.
   Related Arts Team, 11:00-11:42 A.M.

This schedule was in effect for the first and third ten-week periods of the school year. For the second and fourth ten-week periods of the school year the following planning schedule was in effect:

   Team M, 8:45- 9:27 A.M.
   Team I, 9:30-10:12 A.M.
   Team D, 9:30-10:12 A.M.
   Team L, 2:05- 2:50 P.M.

Figure 7-D1
Liverpool Junior High School—First Floor

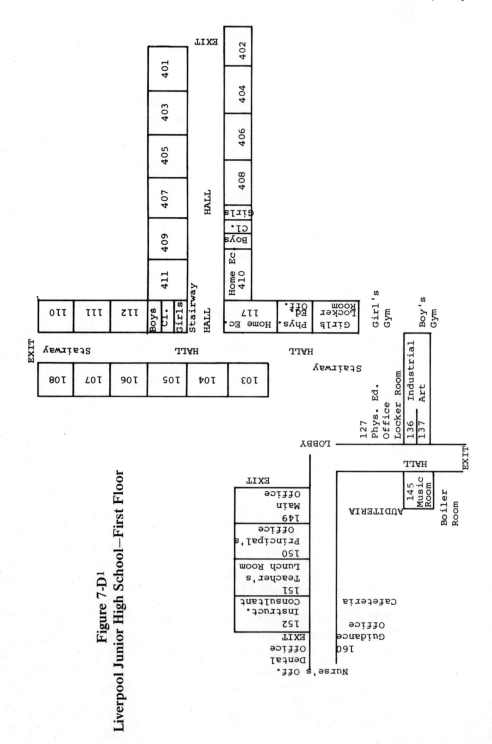

	225 Art	224 Science	223 Reading	Stairway / Girls Closet / Boys	213 Science	Sci. Stor. / Dark Room	215 Science

STAIRWAY   HALL   HALL   STAIRWAY

Curr. Room / Tch. Room	207 Library	Library Wk. Room / Confer. Room	210 Language	211 Language Labs	212 Language Labs	213 Science

Figure 7-D²
Liverpool Junior High School—Second Floor

Team J, 1:15- 2:00 P.M.
Team H, 2:05- 2:50 P.M.
Related Arts Team, 11:45-12:27 P.M.

This flip-flop schedule (see page 92) was employed to bring much needed diversity into student and teacher schedules.

C. The Curriculum Room on the second floor next to the library became the office of the Coordinator of Independent Study and Student Research.

D. Room 103 on the first floor became the new faculty dining room.

E. Room 223 across from the library on the second floor was designated as the English-Social Studies learning center, while room 224 became the Math-Science learning center. The reading center was moved into the old teachers' room on the second floor, next to the office of the independent study coordinator.

F. The auditeria, a combination of a cafeteria and an auditorium, was designated as the student commons center when not in use for lunch.

G. An office was constructed for the teacher aides by making use of hall space adjacent to the main office.

H. The rooms set aside for team instruction were:

Team M — rooms 402, 404, 406, and 218.
Team I — rooms 405, 407, 409, and 215.
Team D — rooms 408, 105, 106, and 213.
Team L — rooms 401, 403, 405, and 218.
Team J — rooms 406, 407, 408, and 215.
Team H — rooms 106, 107, 111, and 213.
Related Arts Team — rooms 410 and 117
for Home Ecomonics; rooms 136 and 137
for Industrial Arts; room 145 for music
and 225 for Art; and rooms 210, 211, and
212 for foreign language.

It must be remembered that, according to the flip-flop master schedule, only three interdisciplinary teams, either M-I-D or L-J-H, were teaching at the same time. All rooms specially equipped for science lab classes were unfortunately built on the second floor, thus the science member of each team was geographically removed from his teammates who were teaching on the first floor.

I. The only two double rooms in the building were 401-403 and 402-404. They were separated by folding partitions. Only one double room was formally assigned to any one team during a three-hour block of time. This always left the other double room available for any teachers who wanted to use it. This facility could house 90 students comfortably. If larger facilities were needed, the auditeria was used.

In the staff's professional judgment, making these adjustments in the use of the school plant enabled the ungraded middle school program to be launched smoothly, efficiently, and effectively despite a traditionally designed building.

Evaluating Teacher and Team Performances

If the principal is to be the educational leader in his building he must evaluate how well each member of his staff is functioning both as an individual and as a member of a team. Since the principal is responsible for the education of the students housed in his building, he must evaluate how effective the different programs and various instructional techniques are with different groups of students. As he makes judgments concerning programs and techniques the building principal is really evaluating the decisions that teachers and teams have made about what they are going to do with their students and how they are going to do it. These professional impressions must be conveyed to the individual staff members both verbally and in writing, with opportunities being given for differences of opinion to be expressed.

At all times however teachers and teams must be judged in terms of the educational objectives of the school and in terms of the professional decision-making opportunities that have been presented to them. Thus some questions to be raised in evaluating a teacher's and/or his team's commitment to the program and thus their effectiveness are:

1. Are opportunities given for students to pursue independent study programs?

2. Is there subgrouping within the class?

3. Are differentiated assignments given within a particular class or are all students expected to complete the same assignment?

4. How frequently are pupils regrouped and on what basis are they regrouped?

5. Is a multitext and a multi-media approach to instruction being used?

6. Does the teacher play a domineering role in the classroom as a dispenser of knowledge or does he encourage active student participation while assuming a semi-subordinate role?

7. Are pre- and post-testing devices used before and after a unit is developed?

8. What creative use is being made of different time modules for instructional purposes?

9. Do the students appear to be interested in the curricular programs being developed?

10. What is the quality of the teacher's relationships with his students?

11. How well does the individual teacher work with his teammates?

All of these questions relate directly to the educational and philosophical environment necessary for the success of the ungraded middle school.

To be able to give complete answers to all of these questions as well as others, the building principal must engage in an intensive evaluation program. This necessitates his visiting classrooms and team planning sessions on both a formal and informal basis. Only in this way will he be able to feel the instructional pulse of the school. This will require the principal to establish a definite timetable each week that will take him into classrooms and team planning periods. He cannot just do this when opportunities arise. He must make a definite time commitment to such an evaluation program, otherwise he will fail as other principals in the past have failed in the area of teacher evaluation.

A study done of selected principals in Oregon, see Figure 7-E, clearly demonstrates

> what can happen when the use of time is not consciously planned. The authorities thought that almost one third of the high school principal's time should be spent for supervision of teachers and improvement of instruction. The high school principals in the study thought that approximately one fourth of their time should be spent for that activity. In actual practice, the principals spent less than one eighth of their time carrying it out. By contrast, the principals actually spent almost twice as much time in office routine as they thought they should.[9]

Therefore it is strongly recommended that the principal schedule at least two formal classroom visitations and at least three informal classroom visits each week, with fewer visitations during a week shortened by vacation periods or holidays. This is the only sure way for him to keep on top of the program.

Each formal classroom visitation must be preceded by a pre-observation conference. The teacher should receive formal notice, see Figure 7-F, of the impending visit and of the request for a meeting prior to the visitation. One or two days' notice should be sufficient. The meeting is scheduled so that the principal may be aware of what the

---

9. Samuel Goldman, *The School Principal* (New York: The Center for Applied Research in Education, Inc., 1966), p. 35.

TABLE 1

Comparisons of Time Spent with Principals'
and Authorities' Opinions as to How Time
Should Be Spent in the Secondary
Principalship[10]

PERCENTAGE OF TIME

Category of Duties	Authorities' Opinions N 29	Principals' Opinions N 204	Actually Spent N 62
Office Routine	9.7	12.9	22.5
Activity Program	8.7	9.2	17.8
Teaching	3.1	5.9	13.0
Supervision of Teachers and Improvement of Instruction	31.0	22.0	12.0
Pupil Personnel	11.1	14.5	8.4
Professional Meetings	5.6	3.7	6.6
Public Relations	9.7	6.7	5.6
Administration of the Plant	4.2	6.4	4.6
Superintendent's Conference	4.1	2.7	2.8
Business Management	5.7	7.8	2.7
School Board	2.1	3.2	2.2
Cafeteria	2.3	2.4	1.1
Transportation	2.8	2.6	0.7

Figure 7–E

Time Analysis of Principal's Functions

teacher has planned for a specific day, why he has decided to do this, and how he plans to evaluate the effectiveness of his work. This will give the principal a basis on which to make his own professional judgments about the teacher's performance in the class he is about to visit. While this is a formalized procedure, every effort should be made by the building principal to keep the tone of the session relaxed. He must convey to the teacher his definite desire to become familiar with and involved in the instructional program.

Having ascertained what the teacher's intentions are, the principal has sufficient information for making valid judgments about the class he is to visit. Using Figures 7-G^1, 7-G^2, and 7-G^3 as a guideline, the observer should make note of items he considers to be important. By remaining in the class for not less than twenty nor more than forty minutes, the

10. Harold V. McAbee, "Time for the Job", *The Bullentin of the National Association of Secondary School Principals,* Vol. 42, No. 236 (March 1958), p. 41.

Dear _____:
           Teacher's Name

I would like to have a pre-observation conference with you in my office at _____ on _____, _____.
           Time   Day   Date

Following our discussion, I will plan to visit one of your classes, after
which, at _____, I would like to have a post-observation confer-
           Time
ence with you.

Your truly,

Robert J. McCarthy, Principal

Figure 7—F

Pre-Observation Conference Notice

principal should have a clear picture of the positive and negative aspects of
the lesson as it affected different students within the class.

Later that day, or at the very latest the next day, the principal and
the teacher should have a lengthy post-observation conference. Here the
building principal must immediately throw the ball in the teacher's lap by
asking him to evaluate the lesson that was observed. The evaluation must
be in terms of specifics, not generalities. On occasions, thought-provoking
questions must be asked of the teacher to cause him to examine more
closely what went on in his classroom. After this the building principal
should reveal his perceptions of the situation, which in turn should be
followed by a positively oriented dialogue between the two parties
concerning future directions to be taken by both the teacher and the
principal. Within one week after the post-observation conference the
teacher should receive his copy of the official classroom visitation report
along with a covering letter, Figure 7-H, that indicates what will happen to
the report.

This formalized procedure will convey to all concerned parties the
principal's professional evaluation of the individual teacher's performance
while at the same time providing the teacher with an opportunity to
disagree with the judgments made. While one must always view the entire
process in a positive fashion, as a means of recording in writing outstanding instructional performances or as a device to pinpoint problem
areas and indicate corrective steps to be taken, the official classroom
observation report form can also serve as written testimony for dismissal

CLASSROOM VISITATION REPORT

Teacher _____   Date _____

Team: _____   Number of students present: _____

Topic _____

I.   *Concepts being developed:*

II.   *Skills stressed in presentation:*

III.   *Instructional techniques employed:*

Figure 7–G1

Official Classroom Observation Report Form–Page 1

IV.   *Nature of student-teacher relationships:*

V.   *Quality of the learning environment:*

VI.   *Recommendations for improvement:*

VII.   *Additional comments:*

Teacher's Signature	Observer's Signature and Position

Figure 7–G2

Official Classroom Observation Report Form–Page 2

1. Pre-observation conference held on _____.
                                                        Date

    General comments made:

2. Post-observation conference held on _____.
                                                         Date

    General comments made:

Figure 7–G[3]
Official Classroom Observation Report Form–Page 3

To: _____

From: Building Principal

Date: _____

Regarding: Attached Observation Visitation Report

Enclosed you will find four copies of the observation report based on my recent visit to your class. Please read the report very carefully. You may keep the original. I am asking you to sign the carbon copies and return them to me. Your signature will indicate merely that you have seen the report. One report will then be placed in your personnel folder, one in my files, and one will be given to the Instructional Consultant.

Should you have any questions concerning the report, please feel free to make this known to me, either verbally or in writing.

Thank you very much for your thoughtful consideration in this matter.

Principal

Figure 7-H
Covering Letter for the Observation Report

---

purposes if an individual teacher, tenured or non-tenured, has failed to perform satisfactorily in meeting the school's educational objectives and the students' needs.

The informal classroom visits should ideally be the result of the teachers inviting the building principal into their classes to view activities that they feel would be of interest to him. As the principal travels around the building and sees interesting things going on in different rooms, he should also feel free to drop into classrooms for a few minutes. A complimentary remark to the teacher and/or his students as he leaves the room, or a brief informal chat with the teacher sometime later in the day, will help to create an environment that welcomes the building principal as a frequent classroom visitor.

If the middle school is committed to a teaming approach to instruction, there is no room for an individual who does not wish to be a member of any team. All members of the staff must realize this condition of employment. While experienced personnel may have been used to operating on a self-contained basis, they must adapt to the school's operational philosophy or seek employment elsewhere. An unwillingness to operate as a member of any team must result in a transfer of that individual to another type of setting within the district or his release. Since the task of the school is the education of its students, teacher preferences for modes of operation must bow to the needs of the students and to the organizational structure of the school. With the aid of an Instructional Consultant, those having difficulty in functioning as members of a team can receive advice and assistance in adjusting to this new instructional role.

The effectiveness of a team can be judged by many criteria such as:

1. How many students express a desire to transfer from the team during the course of the year.

2. Student and parental reactions to programs developed by the team.

3. The number of students from that team that pursue independent study programs throughout the year.

4. How frequently and on what basis it groups and regroups its pupils.

5. The quality and the interrelatedness of the instructional programs developed by the team.

6. The manner in which it ascertains student interests and evaluates pupil progress.

7. How cohesive a unit it is and how members help one another in making decisions.

8. Whether any member of a team expresses a desire to transfer to another team.

9. How closely it works with the guidance counselor assigned to it.

10. What transpires during team planning sessions.

Periodically the building principal must assess the effectiveness of each of the teams in his school. From his own personal observations and from discussions with the other members of the leadership team, he will know which teams are effective, which ones are having some difficulties, and which ones are not functioning as a team. He must praise those teams that are functioning well and at the same time encourage them to achieve new goals with their students. Together with the I. C. and the Pupil Personnel Consultant, he must use a variety of approaches to help teams in difficulty. This may mean talking to individual teachers and to entire teams in an attempt to pinpoint problems. If the individuals involved are agreeable to it, personnel may have to be shifted from one team to another to alter the situation. This must only be done with the consent of the majority of those involved.

If a member of a team is attempting to sabotage the entire teaming operation and refuses to follow the recommendations of the building principal or other members of the leadership team, he must, when all reasonable avenues for resolving the matter have been thoroughly explored, be faced with the reality of the situation regardless of his tenure status. The principal must explain the alternatives to him. Either the teacher—

A.   Begins to function as a member of a team;

B.   Transfers to another school in the district that will accept him;

C.   Leaves the district; or

D.   Faces charges of either insubordination or incompetence to function in the new educational setting.

This should indicate to the staff the principal's commitment to helping teachers make the teaming approach to instruction an effective reality.

Keeping Apprised of Instructional Programs

The curriculums that are being developed within different teams and the instructional practices employed daily by members of the professional staff are the key ingredients in the middle school's growth. They will determine how well the needs of the student population are met. While every team member plans specific activities for different classes and different groups within classes on a daily basis, it is also imperative that long-range goals be formulated with and for different students. It is also essential that these long-range goals be communicated to colleagues on other teaching teams. For this reason a plan should be developed to keep all members of the middle school staff apprised of the latest curricular programs being planned. A form entitled "curriculum perspectives" is a device strongly recommended to solve this communications problem.

At regular intervals throughout the school year, each member of the professional staff should be asked to complete a curriculum perspective sheet, see Figure 7-I, for each of their major instructional groups. This very brief form should list the concepts or ideas to be developed within each major instructional group as well as the skill areas that are going to be stressed. In addition to this, the individual teacher is requested to note any items that might be of special interest to other teachers, guidance counselors, the Instructional Consultant, or the building principal, such as instructional techniques that in the past have proven to be effective or audio-visual media that have previously aroused student interest.

These reports should be submitted to the building principal who will analyze and discuss them with the Instructional Consultant and the Coordinator of Independent Study and Student Research. The curriculum perspectives should then be compiled, photocopied, and distributed to the entire staff. This should represent the school's total educational efforts. After the different curriculum perspectives have been read and analyzed, the entire staff should be able to discuss more intelligently what is going

CURRICULUM PERSPECTIVES

Teacher's Last Name	First Name	Date	
Subject	Team	From-Date	To-Date

Concepts or Ideas Being Developed:

1. _____
2. _____
3. _____
4. _____
5. _____

Skills being stressed:

1. _____
2. _____
3. _____
4. _____
5. _____

Items of Interest:

1. _____
2. _____

Figure 7–I
Curriculum Perspectives Sheet

on in their middle school since they will now be aware of what their colleagues are planning to do.

No teacher however should be expected to complete the curriculum perspectives sheet until he has had an opportunity to know his students. Therefore this form should not be completed for the first time until the end of the second or third week of school. This should give teachers and teams sufficient time to get to know their students and to develop some long-range goals for different instructional groups. The first such perspective sheet might therefore cover a period of time from the third through the eighth week of school. Prior to completing a second series of curriculum perspective sheets covering perhaps a period of time from the ninth through the fourteenth week of school, teachers and teams should be asked to analyze and compare their previously established goals with what was actually achieved. This self-analysis can help the staff to establish more realistic goals for itself and its students.

The Principal's Role in Disciplinary Matters

When rapidly changing young adolescents are faced with rigid, inflexible, depersonalized schools, many discipline problems are bound to erupt. But when the building principal creates an organizational structure based on an interdisciplinary teaming concept and gives staff opportunities to develop programs that meet the intellectual, social, emotional, and physical needs of its students, fewer discipline cases will arise. By allowing students to elect certain courses of study, by providing them with opportunities to pursue independent research, and by abolishing formalized study halls and replacing them with a student commons relaxation center, the principal has taken steps to create an environment within the school that appeals to youngsters of this age.

It is vital to the success of the ungraded middle school that previous errors in early adolescent education not be repeated, especially with regards to student fads and fancies.

Issues must not be made over small things such as gum chewing, or over items that can become a *cause celebre* such as student dress or political activity. If the school is to create a climate where students feel that teachers and administrators are sincerely interested in them and in their education, then forms of punishment such as detention and suspension must be replaced, where possible, by a more personalized approach to the problem. Suspensions should be used only as a last resort, and then only as a means to bring the parents to school to discuss the problem. Principals should establish a procedure similar to most grievance procedures wherein attempts are made to resolve problems at the lowest possible level—that is, between teacher and student.[11]

---

11. Robert J. McCarthy, "Minimizing Disciplinary Problems by Humanizing the School", *Middle School/Junior High Principal's Service* (New London, Connecticut: Croft Educational Services, Inc., August, 1970), p. 4.

From this author's professional experience with middle schools in urban and suburban settings that have been organized on an ungraded, interdisciplinary basis, disciplinary problems needing the principal's attention are reduced by at least 50 percent. Most are resolved internally, by the teams with their students. Many never develop because of the environment prevailing throughout the school.

But when problems do develop that a teacher or a team cannot resolve successfully, such as open hostility between a student and one of his teachers, the principal should be contacted immediately. As an authority figure he must take immediate action to restore order and respect, while "saving face" for both parties. He must then meet individually with the student and with the teacher to get their views and feelings on the incident. Only after all the data has been gathered and the parties heard, should the principal render a decision as to an appropriate resolution of the problem. His decision must be based on the facts and take into account the feelings of both student and teacher.

Other Job Demands

It is absolutely essential that the building principal establish good relationships with students, teachers, central office personnel, and members of the community. He must be an individual rather than an office, always available to clarify areas of concern, ready to act with firmness when necessary, and constantly endeavoring to sell his ideas and those of his staff.

He must work hard to convince students that he is not the demon they expect, nor a pushover. Constant visibility can show him to be friendly, firm, and fair. The manner in which the building principal handles important disciplinary matters, and the way he educates staff to deal with similar problems will convey this positive message to the students. If he is seen in classrooms participating in group discussions, if he visits the student commons to talk with youngsters, and if he occasionally eats lunch with them, students will respect him and view the school as a friendly, personalized place where they can achieve a certain degree of success.

The middle school principal must also be able to adapt to the different personalities and idiosyncrasies of his co-workers on the staff. In essence he must do that which he expects of his teachers, that is, be supportive, impartial, and open to suggestions. His degree of adaptability and flexibility will determine how well the individual teachers and teams function.

With the creation of the ungraded middle school as described throughout this book, many new programs and instructional techniques should be developed. It is therefore essential that central office personnel, especially the superintendent, the assistant superintendent for instruction, and the director of secondary education, be continually apprised of the latest developments within the school. At meetings of the superintendent's council, the principal should mention those items he feels will be of interest to the other administrators in the district. He should also feel free to call upon directors in such special areas as Art and Music to work cooperatively with his staff in an advisory capacity on curriculum projects.

Community relationships are best fostered by the attitudes that students convey to their parents and friends about the school they attend. Although regular monthly meetings should be scheduled in cooperation with the local parents' association on items of mutual interest to both teachers and taxpayers, if the students are happy in school and are demonstrating their growth intellectually and socially to adults, the school will have a positive image in the eyes of the community. It is also advisable to schedule parent visitation days, report card conferences, meetings between individual instructional teams and fifteen to twenty parents, and regular publicity releases to continuously keep the public informed of student and teacher successes. Unless time is spent in what may sometimes seem like an endless series of meetings with these groups, the ungraded middle school cannot succeed. The building principal must take definite steps to establish firm, positive ties with each of these four distinct, concerned groups.

Summary

Because of the demands made upon the individual and the office, the building principalship is a hotspot today. This chapter has explored in depth the qualities that the principal of an ungraded middle school must possess to fulfill the duties and responsibilities of the position. The necessity of his sharing specific decision-making prerogatives with teachers, students, and members of the building leadership team, the importance of his developing sound budgetary procedures that reflect the school's educational plans, and his creative use of existing physical facilities, both old and new, were analyzed. Formalized procedures were also suggested for evaluating individual teacher and team performances, for keeping apprised of contemplated instructional programs, and for handling situations that are often referred to as disciplinary matters. Finally the principal's relationships with students, teachers, central office personnel, and the community were discussed along with positive measures to establish firm ties with each of these groups.

Chapter 8

The Middle School
Guidance Program

BECAUSE THE UNGRADED middle school is child-centered in its
approach to curriculum development and instructional techniques,
guidance counselors must play a vital role in its operations. But if the
middle school guidance program is to succeed and have a positive effect
on students, staff, and community, then guidance counselors will have to
play new roles, quite different from the manner in which they have
functioned in most traditional junior high schools.

This chapter will focus on the counselor's relationships with teachers
and teaching teams and on their function of assigning students to specific
teaching teams. The necessity for classroom visitations by counselors is
explored along with the need for their attendance at team planning
sessions. Systems devised to report pupil progress that are consistent with
the school's educational philosophy are analyzed along with errors to be
avoided in initiating new reporting practices. The chapter concludes with a
discussion of how middle school students can be prepared for entrance
into high school and how the high school can prepare itself for the middle
school students.

Relationships with Teachers and Teams

Too often in the past guidance counselors have, either by intent or
through omission, separated themselves from the teaching staff. The very

location of their offices, generally in the administrative wing of the building, often physically removed them from convenient contact with teachers on a daily basis. Staff thus began to view counselors as semi-administrative personnel. Their notions were reinforced as more and more counselors were appointed to fill administrative positions within the system. As a result the position of guidance counselor was viewed by many as merely a stepping-stone. This caused many teachers to demean the role of the counselor in the building.

To counteract this prevailing point of view each middle school guidance counselor must make a concerted effort to have more direct, daily contact with teachers and teaching teams. The counselor must sell himself and his services to the staff. This can be done in a number of ways, but perhaps it can best be accomplished when the counselor displays confidence in the teaching teams with which he works. For example, student folders containing test scores, psychological data, results of parent conferences, and previous report cards, traditionally have been kept under tight security in the guidance office. If teachers wanted access to this information they had to go to that office. Often they were not allowed to remove the files from the guidance office to study them in a more relaxed environment elsewhere in the building. Frequently certain information was not even found in the student's folder but was filed separately and not shared with the teachers because of the so-called "confidential nature" of the material. This type of approach by the guidance department tended to create the impression that teachers were either not to be trusted with this information or else they were not sophisticated enough to comprehend it.

By removing the student folders from the guidance office and putting them in the appropriate interdisciplinary team planning rooms, vital information is placed where it can have the greatest use and be of the greatest benefit to both students and teachers. Teachers are then bound to make use of the material contained in these folders in a professional, discriminating manner. The counselor, when he wants specific information about a student, must then go to the team's planning room to secure this material where he will frequently come into contact with the youngster's teachers.

With this approach teams will find it more convenient to bring problems to the counselor's attention which they themselves will not be able to resolve. Since many of the problems that early adolescents are faced with can be handled by the interdisciplinary teams because of the relationships they establish with their students over a two- or three-year span of time, the guidance counselor's expertise can then be used to handle those situations that the team cannot cope with alone. This however does not mean that the counselor handles deep-seated emotional problems. This must be the sole province of the school psychologist or psychiatrist, not the guidance counselor.

Aside from working closely with those students who need his help, the counselor must continually serve the needs of teachers by contacting parents, making arrangements for parent-team conferences, summarizing what transpired at these meetings, helping teachers to develop diagnostic testing devices, and aiding them in interpreting the various stanine and precentile results of standardized testing programs. Thus a positive relationship will be created and fostered between teachers and counselors which will have a beneficial effect on the operations of the middle school.

For guidance to function effectively there should be one guidance counselor for every three interdisciplinary teams. This means that the student-counselor ratio may range from 300 to 375 to 1 depending upon the number of students assigned to each team. While this is considerably higher than the ratios suggested by professional guidance associations, it is a very workable figure since many time-consuming functions traditionally performed by counselors in departmentalized junior high schools such as grouping and scheduling, will now be handled by the interdisciplinary teams themselves.

Just as teaching teams must be formed on the basis of the desires of individuals to work together, and students must be assigned to the team with which they will learn best, so must guidance counselors be assigned to specific teams with which it appears they will be able to work in concert. This is essential if the counselors are to work closely and successfully with their assigned teaching teams.

Assigning Students to Teams

The ungraded middle school as described throughout this book is based on an interdisciplinary, conceptual approach to instruction. Therefore one of the most important functions that guidance will be responsible for is concerned with the placement of each youngster with the interdisciplinary teaching team that will best meet his needs. This must be done if teachers and students are to work well together and achieve goals made possible within this new organizational framework.

Once the composition of each interdisciplinary team has been determined, it is obvious that no two teams will be alike. Each will have its own unique characteristics due to the personnel on it. It therefore simply becomes a matter of having the guidance counselors and the other members of the leadership team examine pertinent data on each student to determine his team placement. In a 650 pupil school it should take approximately four weeks during the summer to complete this task, averaging slightly better than 150 placements per week, 30 to 35 per day. This operation should involve a team of five professionals: the building principal, the Instructional Consultant, the Coordinator of Independent Study and Student Research, the Pupil Personnel Consultant, and the other guidance counselor. Each member of the team should examine each student's folder.

In the Liverpool Middle School, Liverpool, New York, it was decided by the building leadership team, prior to the placement of students with teams, that:

1. a team composed mainly of teachers with less than three years' experience would not have students that were either extremely talented or extremely handicapped;

2. each team would handle at least two grade levels, with some exceptional teams handling students from levels six, seven and eight;

3. teams that were somewhat "traditional" in their make-up would deal primarily with students who had not yet acquired many of their basic skills in any number of areas; and

4. teams that were termed "experimental" would work with pupils who already possessed many of the basic skills needed to achieve success in the various disciplines.[1]

In order to further personalize and humanize the entire team placement and scheduling operation, middle school teachers were asked in January to develop a series of questions dealing with background information that they would like to know about the elementary students who would be entering the middle school the following September. Figures 8-A through 8-G illustrate the results of their efforts. In March these questionnaires were distributed to the elementary teachers of these students. Within three months this data was returned to the middle school guidance counselors who had an opportunity to analyze the material and resolve unclear areas with the elementary guidance counselors and teachers.

This data, combined with other material contained in the youngsters' guidance folders pertaining to such areas as:

1. Family background,
2. Individual interests,
3. Past academic success,
4. Health records,
5. Mental maturity scores,
6. Present achievement scores, and
7. Notes summarizing parental conferences,

---

1. Robert J. McCarthy, *How to Organize and Operate an Ungraded Middle School* (Englewood Cliffs, New Jersey: Prentice-Hall, Inc., 1967), pp. 28-29.

Pupil's Last Name _____ First Name _____ Sex _____ Age _____

General Questions

1. Is this student generally able to see relationships between facts or incidents?

 Yes _____

 No _____

2. Is this student mature or immature for his age?

 Mature _____

 Immature _____

3. Has the student given any evidence of having any emotional problems?

 Yes _____

 No _____

4. Has this student proven to be a discipline problem?

 Yes _____

 No _____

5. Does this student usually demonstrate responsibility by handing work in on time?

 Yes _____

 No _____

6. Can this student recognize a problem when faced with one?

 Yes _____

 No _____

7. Is this student an active participant in your classes?

 Yes _____

 No _____

8. Has this child demonstrated any particular signs of creativity?

 Yes _____

 No _____

9. Does this student generally know how to go about solving problems?

 Yes _____

 No _____

10. Does this child have any speech impairments?

 Yes _____

 No _____

11. Would this child profit from being placed in a self-contained environment, that is, one teacher instructing the pupil in most of his subjects?

 Yes _____

 No _____

12. Is this child really capable of pursuing independent study in an area?

 Yes _____

 No _____

 If YES, which one _____

Figure 8–A
Student Background Data

13. Does this child have any rather noticeable physical impairments?
    Yes _____
    No _____

14. Are there any students who should not be in the same class as this student?
    Yes _____
    No _____

    If Yes, please list names:
    _____
    _____

15. Does this student need a very structured classroom environment to really have learning take place?
    Yes _____
    No _____

16. Has this student developed notetaking skills?
    Yes _____
    No _____

17. Are there any social factors in this child's background that might affect his learning in the classroom?
    Yes _____
    No _____

18. Does this child have a poor attitude toward school and learning?
    Yes _____
    No _____

19. In what area or areas of study could this child most use some extra help?
    A _____ B _____
    C _____

20. Does this student know how to use a library?
    Yes _____
    No _____

21. Are his resource work and reference material generally limited to encyclopedias?
    Yes _____
    No _____

22. Does this child know how to "use" a textbook?
    Yes _____
    No _____

23. Does this child know "how" to study?
    Yes _____
    No _____

24. Does this student have the ability to recognize and distinguish main ideas from supporting thoughts?
    Yes _____
    No _____

25. Does this child use correct spelling in his daily work?
    Yes _____
    No _____

Figure 8–B
Student Background Data

26. Is this student easily distracted?

Yes _____

No _____

27. Please rate this child's motivation. (check one)

A. Highly motivated   A _____
B. Effectively motivated B _____
C. Usually purposeful   C _____
D. Vacillating   D _____
E. Purposeless   E _____

28. Please rate this child's integrity. (check one)

A. Very trustworthy   A _____
B. Generally honest   B _____
C. Questionable at times C _____
D. Not dependable   D _____

29. Please rate this person's industry. (check one)

A. Seeks extra work   A _____
B. Assigned work done regularly B _____
C. Needs periodic prodding   C _____
D. Needs constant reminders   D _____
E. Seldom does any work   E _____

30. Is this pupil capable of abstract reasoning?

Yes _____

No _____

31. Please rate this pupil's ability level in each of the following areas. (check one in each area)

English

A. Excellent   A _____
B. Good   B _____
C. Fair   C _____
D. Poor   D _____

Social Studies

A. Excellent   A _____
B. Good   B _____
C. Fair   C _____
D. Poor   D _____

Reading Information

1. Has this student demonstrated any reading problems?

Yes _____

No _____

2. Is this student reading above, at, or below grade level? (check one)

Above _____

At _____

Below _____

3. How would you rate this child's reading ability? (check one)

A. Excellent   A _____   C. Fair   C _____
B. Good   B _____   D. Poor   D _____

Figure 8–C
Student Background Data

4. How would you rate this child's comprehension ability? (check one)

A. Excellent A _____   C. Fair C _____
B. Good B _____   D. Poor D _____

5. How would you rate this child's ability to express in writing?

A. Excellent A _____   C. Fair C _____
B. Good B _____   D. Poor D _____

6. Does this individual like to read?

Yes _____
No _____

7. Does this student read at different speeds according to the type of material he is reading?

Yes _____
No _____

8. Is this child currently receiving remedial reading instruction?

Yes _____
No _____

9. Check the following word attack skills which this student uses proficiently:

phonetics _____   structural analysis _____
context _____   dictionary _____

10. At what so-called "grade level" is this child now reading? _____

Foreign Language Information

1. Please rate this child's listening ability. (check one)

A. Excellent A _____   D. Fair D _____
B. Very Good B _____   E. Poor E _____
C. Good C _____

2. Please rate this child's "mimicry" ability. (check one)

A. Excellent A _____   D. Fair D _____
B. Very Good B _____   E. Poor E _____
C. Good C _____

3. Please rate this child's ability to memorize? (check one)

A. Excellent A _____   D. Fair D _____
B. Very Good B _____   E. Poor E _____
C. Good C _____

4. Please rate this child's "retention" ability? (check one)

A. Excellent A _____   D. Fair D _____
B. Very Good B _____   E. Poor E _____
C. Good C _____

Figure 8–D
Student Background Data

5. Would this child benefit from being exposed to a foreign language next year?
   Yes ———
   No ———

6. Should (in your estimation) this child take a foreign language next year?
   Yes ———
   No ———

7. At this point, do you feel that the student would take French or Spanish?
   French ———
   Spanish ———
   Undecided ———

Mathematics Information

1. Has this student been exposed to modern math?
   Yes ———
   No ———

2. Is the basic approach now being used in his mathematics termed to be the "traditional" approach or the "modern math" approach?
   Traditional ———
   Modern ———

3. Does this student "like" math?
   Yes ———
   No ———

4. Does this student "dislike" math?
   Yes ———
   No ———

5. As of the completion date of this form, what are the last 4 areas that this student has covered?
   A. ———
   B. ———
   C. ———
   D. ———

6. Is one single textbook being used by this student in the area of math?
   Yes ———
   No ———

   If YES, which one? ———

7. At what "grade level" in math would you say that this child is now operating?

A. Third	A ———	E. Seventh	E ———
B. Fourth	B ———	F. Eighth	F ———
C. Fifth	C ———	G. Ninth	G ———
D. Sixth	D ———	H. Tenth	H ———

8. Is this student capable of pursuing some type of independent study in the area of math?
   Yes ———
   No ———

9. Does this child have any fundamental weakness in math?
   Yes ———
   No ———

   If YES, please comment:

Figure 8–E
Student Background Data

10. Please rate this pupil's ability level in the area of math? (check one)

A. Excellent   A _____   C. Fair   C _____
B. Good   B _____   D. Poor   D _____

Science Information

1. This student's science classes met _____ times per week. Each class lasted for approximately _____ minutes.

2. The approach mainly used was: (check one)

A. Lecture   A _____
B. Discussion   B _____
C. Teacher demonstration C _____
D. Student experimentation D _____

3. The area of science that was given the greatest emphasis in the course was:

A. Biology   A _____   C. Earth Science   C _____
B. Chemistry B _____   D. Physics   D _____

4. Does the student have an interest in science?

Yes _____
No _____

5. Does the student have the ability to do well in science?

Yes _____
No _____

6. Was one single textbook used in teaching this course?

Yes _____
No _____

If YES, which text? _____
If YES, was the basic format of the textbook followed?

Yes _____
No _____

7. Does this student have the ability to read and understand scientific information?

Yes _____
No _____

8. Does the student have the ability to manipulate simple lab equipment:

Yes _____
No _____

9. Is this pupil capable of pursuing independent study in the area of science?

Yes _____
No _____

Figure 8–F
Student Background Data

10. Please rate this pupil's ability level in the area of science.
    (check one)

    A. Excellent   A _____   C. Fair   C _____
    B. Good   B _____   D. Poor   D _____

11. Does this student have the ability to draw valid con-
    clusions from his observations of an experiment or dem-
    onstration?   Yes _____
                                         No _____

12. Would this student pose a danger to himself and to others
    in a laboratory situation?   Yes _____
                                        No _____

Important Comments:

Figure 8–G

Student Background Data

---

served as a good basis for student placement with interdisciplinary teams.
The first year that this procedure was used in the Liverpool Middle School
there were only ten student requests for transfer to other teams. This was
due in large measure to the meticulous care with which records were
analyzed and judgments made.

Counselors Must Visit Classrooms

If a guidance counselor is to be able to intelligently discuss, with a
parent or teacher, a student's classroom behavior or a teacher's instructional relationship with a certain youngster, the counselor must have
direct, firsthand experience to support his recommendations. This can
only be obtained by spending time in classrooms observing the operational patterns. Only in this way can the counselor discuss, with any
degree of accuracy, what is taking place in the learning environment.

Too often in the past counselors have talked with parents in
generalities. This was because the counselors did not have actual knowledge of what was taking place in different classrooms. They received
feedback from students as they talked with them in the guidance suite.

Counselors occasionally heard about problem students from teachers. But from a source standpoint, this was secondary or tertiary information. To really be of assistance, the counselor must have access to primary sources. In this case the primary source of information is the classroom where students and teachers act, react, and interact.

Therefore in order to be better able to counsel students, advise parents, and help teachers, guidance counselors must feel free to visit classrooms to observe how their counselees:

A. Function in a typical classroom setting;
B. Respond to teacher-initiated questions;
C. Work in small groups;
D. Follow directions;
E. Function on their own;
F. Handle a test or a quiz;
G. Get along with their peer group; and
H. Make inquiries of their teachers.

Naturally great care must be exercised by the counselor so that neither the student nor the teacher feels that he is being examined under a microscope. But the more a counselor is seen in the classroom the less he will be noticed and the more his presence will be accepted. Such a program must of course initially be introduced to staff by the building principal and its purpose clearly explained in detail. It must be stressed that the counselor is there to serve both the needs of the students and the teachers and that his occasional presence in classrooms can help him fulfill his duties and responsibilities to both parties. Only direct classroom experiences will provide guidance counselors with data necessary for them to make recommendations to students, teachers, and parents that will have a beneficial effect on the operations of the school.

Attendance at Team Planning Sessions

With each guidance counselor being assigned to specific interdisciplinary teams, it is imperative that they attend at least one planning session of each of their teams every week. At some of these meetings the counselor should be prepared to simply listen and note, not only what each individual member of the team is doing in his particular subject matter area, but also the overall approach of the team. He should become familiar with each team's:

1. Grouping patterns and the rationale for them,
2. Instructional programs,
3. Types of homework assignments,
4. Approaches to discipline,

5. Use of the instructional time block, and
6. Student evaluation practices.

If there are points that are not clear to him, the counselor must ask the team to clarify these areas. The knowledge gained from attending these planning sessions will give the counselor a sound basis for responding to parental inquiries and student concerns about the educational programs and instructional techniques being developed by the respective teams.

At other team meetings the counselor must be prepared to discuss specific students and the problems they present to the team. The counselor may ask the team members to share with him their comments and observations regarding a particular student. The initial impetus for the discussion may stem from a telephone call from a parent or from a conference with a student. On other occasions the team may ask for the counselor's advice about dealing with a certain youngster and may ask him to make specific recommendations on a course of action for the team to follow.

When guidance counselors attend team planning sessions on a regular basis and discuss both students and instructional programs with the members of the team, both parties generally come away from the meeting with a better understanding of the problems that each faces. As counselors follow up these meetings with classroom visitations to observe specific students in action, they have more background information on both the student and the team. This additional data, frequently unavailable to guidance counselors operating in the time-honored manner of traditionally graded schools, can make the counselor a far more effective member of the middle school staff.

Reporting Pupil Progress

If the ungraded middle school is to meet the individual needs of its students by developing different instructional programs, it is essential that a reporting system be employed that reports not only a student's growth in various subject matter areas, but also indicates the different, specific curricular programs that he has pursued in each discipline. As was pointed out in the third chapter, the phrase "curricular programs" refers to those topics, skills, or concepts, recently stressed with the student. Such a curriculum record should be an invaluable aid to future teachers in their program planning. Armed with a written record of what the student has pursued and successfully completed, teachers can more accurately develop curricular programs designed to capitalize on skills previously mastered and concepts already grasped. It is strongly recommended by this author that such a curriculum record be included, along with measures of student growth, as an integral part of the middle school's reporting system.

It is obvious that the typical IBM type of report card cannot fulfill this need. Bubbles and checklists are not the answer. Letter or number grades are not sufficient by themselves. The answer lies in a reporting system that:

1. Conveys to parents the curricular program that their child recently pursued in each discipline;

2. Indicates to future teachers the different programs that the student has completed along with an assessment of the youngster's strengths and weaknesses;

3. Takes note of the student's present ability in each discipline area as revealed by diagnostic tests employed by the teacher;

4. Recognizes and evaluates each youngster's growth in terms of his ability in each subject matter area;

5. Is sent home by each teacher at a time when he feels that it is appropriate to communicate the student's growth to both the parent and the pupil; and

6. Can be used by all personnel, thus insuring uniformity in reporting practices.

In the Liverpool Junior High School, letter grade report cards were traditionally sent home every ten weeks. A student received a mark on the card from each of his teachers. Although parents received some indication from the letter grades as to how their son or daughter was doing in each subject matter area, they knew little about the instructional programs their youngster was pursuing. When the 7-8-9 junior high became a 6-7-8 ungraded middle school organized on an interdisciplinary teaming basis, some staff members wondered why they had to be saddled with a rigid, outmoded report card.

Encouraged by the building leadership team to develop a new reporting system more consistent with the middle school's philosophy, these staff members requested and received permission to use a superintendent's conference day to study the problem with the entire staff. Figure 8-H illustrates the reporting device they developed, commonly referred to as the continuous progress report. This was ultimately adopted by the district and used in all its middle schools.

The use of this form, which was to be completed and sent home by a teacher when one of his students had completed a unit of work, meant that parents would be receiving a series of reports throughout the entire year from different teachers, rather than just a single report from all teachers at four definite times during the year. It was felt that if each teacher was free to send home a continuous progress report at intervals throughout the year as indicated by the individual student's growth, no staff member would feel obligated to send them all out at the same time

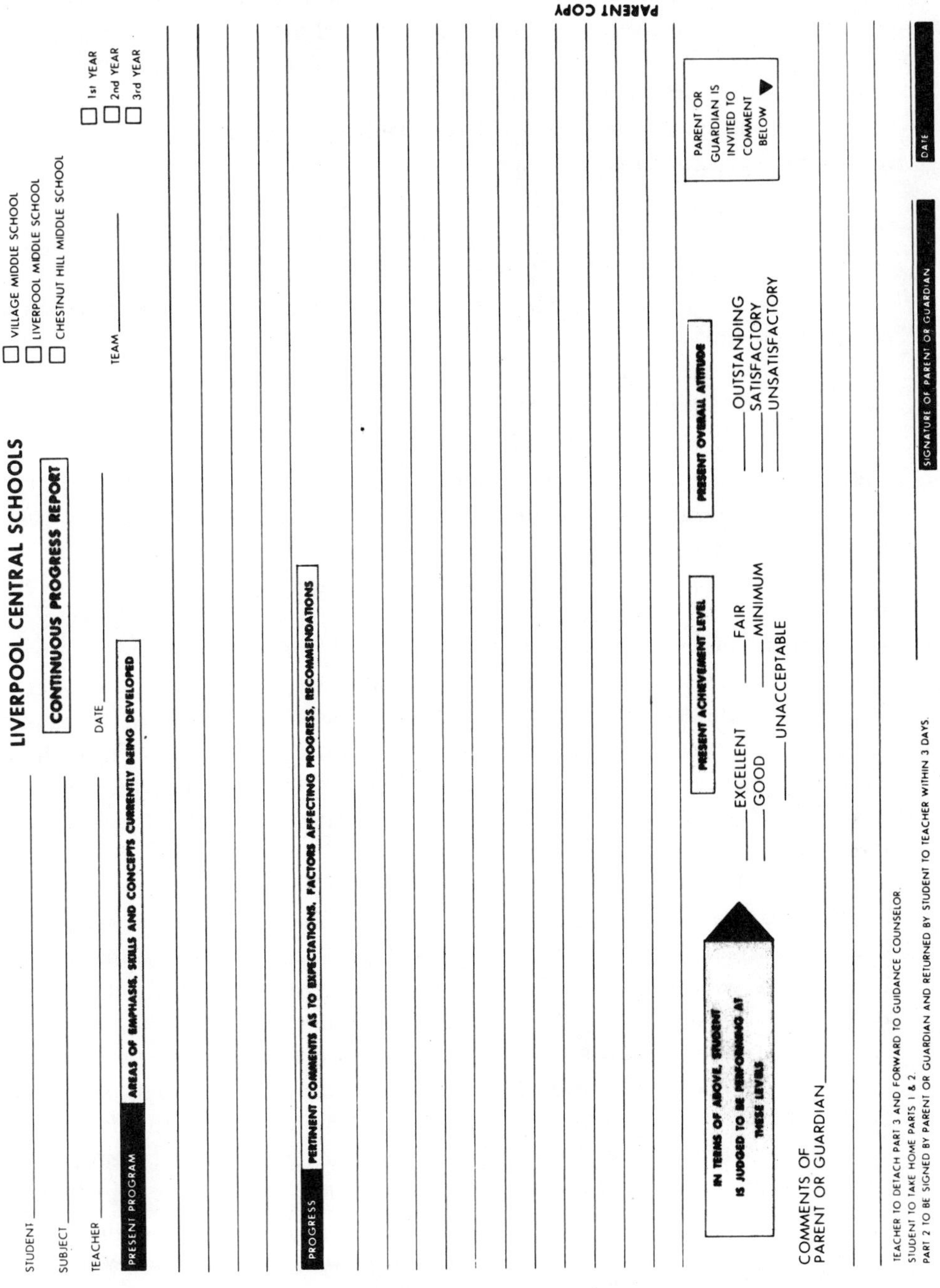

PARENT COPY

LIVERPOOL CENTRAL SCHOOLS

CONTINUOUS PROGRESS REPORT

☐ VILLAGE MIDDLE SCHOOL
☐ LIVERPOOL MIDDLE SCHOOL
☐ CHESTNUT HILL MIDDLE SCHOOL

☐ 1st YEAR
☐ 2nd YEAR
☐ 3rd YEAR

STUDENT _____

SUBJECT _____

TEACHER _____

DATE _____   TEAM _____

PRESENT PROGRAM   AREAS OF EMPHASIS, SKILLS AND CONCEPTS CURRENTLY BEING DEVELOPED

PROGRESS   PERTINENT COMMENTS AS TO EXPECTATIONS, FACTORS AFFECTING PROGRESS, RECOMMENDATIONS

IN TERMS OF ABOVE, STUDENT IS JUDGED TO BE PERFORMING AT THESE LEVELS

PRESENT ACHIEVEMENT LEVEL
___ EXCELLENT
___ GOOD
___ FAIR
___ MINIMUM
___ UNACCEPTABLE

PRESENT OVERALL ATTITUDE
___ OUTSTANDING
___ SATISFACTORY
___ UNSATISFACTORY

PARENT OR GUARDIAN IS INVITED TO COMMENT BELOW ▶

COMMENTS OF PARENT OR GUARDIAN _____

SIGNATURE OF PARENT OR GUARDIAN _____   DATE _____

TEACHER TO DETACH PART 3 AND FORWARD TO GUIDANCE COUNSELOR
STUDENT TO TAKE HOME PARTS 1 & 2.
PART 2 TO BE SIGNED BY PARENT OR GUARDIAN AND RETURNED BY STUDENT TO TEACHER WITHIN 3 DAYS

Figure 8-H
Liverpool Middle School Continuous Progress Report

on all his students. With fewer reports to complete at any one time, each teacher could give more analysis and individual attention to each report. As a safeguard for the project, each teacher had to complete a minimum of four reports on each of his students during the year, with at least one report sent home during each ten-week evaluation period.

The "present program" portion of the continuous progress report was devoted to the curricular program that the student had recently pursued. In this section the teacher was expected to include:

A.   The goals that the student and teacher had formulated;

B.   The extent to which specific concepts had been explored or skills developed; and

C.   The instructional techniques that were used to achieve the previously established goals such as independent study or small group discussions.

Parents thus received a detailed picture of the instructional program that their child was pursuing during the weeks that had passed since the last report was received.

The second phase of the continuous progress report used in Liverpool focused on the growth that the individual student was making in terms of his previously described instructional program. Ample space was provided on the form itself so that a teacher could comment on each student's strengths and weaknesses. Staff was also encouraged to make specific recommendations, when necessary, to parents as to how they might reinforce the school's efforts to help their child. Teachers would also mention steps that they would undertake to help the student improve.

At the bottom of the continuous progress report form teachers were to indicate the present achievement level of the student in terms of his ability in that phase of the subject matter area recently studied. The teacher was also asked to indicate the student's attitude in his class. The form also left space for the parent to correspond with the teacher.

The continuous progress report form used in Liverpool was developed in cooperation with Moore Business Forms, Inc. Using mark sensitive paper, the teacher, when completing a report, automatically had two additional copies made on color-coded paper. Form one (white), the parent's copy, and form two (yellow), the teacher's copy, were sent home. The student was to return the signed yellow copy to the teacher who issued the report. The parent kept the white copy. The third copy, a pink form, was forwarded to the guidance counselor.

Errors to be Avoided in Reporting

The one major fault of the previously described continuous progress report was that it contained no space for a letter or numerical grade indicating the student's progress. Parents, conditioned by years of experience to a letter or a number on a report card, wanted to be informed in these terms which were familiar to them. This form, while conveying a great deal of information, was not sufficient for their needs. When parents saw no grade on the form, they were concerned and anxious.

Several school district's have solved this problem by substituting a letter or numerical grade in place of the excellent, good, fair, minimum, or unacceptable heading under the present achievement level column while at the same time conveying the more significant information to parents about their child's curricular program and his progress in it.

High School Preparation

A successful ungraded middle school is bound to cause turmoil for traditionally oriented high schools and their teachers. Middle school students and teachers must not however be handicapped by predetermined curricular programs designed merely to satisfy the needs of high school teachers and administrators. The high school must be held accountable for meeting the needs of the entering middle school students. Central office personnel, with the support of the board of education, must see to it that the faculty of the high school develops instructional programs appropriate for students coming from the ungraded middle school, regardless of their age-grade-level designation. Programs must be offered on the elementary and middle school level as well as on the college level depending upon the students' previous level of achievement, irrespective of the preconceived expectations of high school teachers and administrators.

Steps must therefore be taken to inform all high school personnel of the different curricular programs that students have been exposed to in previous years. The previously discussed continuous progress reports, which should be forwarded to high school personnel involved with both scheduling and program development, can be of tremendous benefit in achieving this goal.

It is quite apparent that high schools must revamp their traditional organizational structures and operational procedures to give staff some of the same freedom and responsibility accorded middle school personnel. Only in this way will the high school be able to meet the needs of the incoming students.

Summary

If middle school guidance counselors are to be successful they must work closely with both teaching teams and the students assigned to each team. This chapter has presented several plans that can help counselors play a more vital role in the school's operation.

When student records are transferred to the offices of the teaching teams, when counselors initiate and maintain all contacts with parents, and when students are placed with teaching teams for definite reasons rather than simply by chance, the counselors will have a greater positive influence on the school. To further increase his effectiveness, the counselor must also attend team planning sessions to learn of the curricular programs being developed. He then must visit classrooms to see how these programs are directly affecting his counselees.

It is also essential that the ungraded middle school develop a system of reporting students' growth to parents that is in keeping with the school's educational philosophy. The continuous progress report is a system that fulfills this need while also providing future teachers with vital information on the wide range of previous accomplishments of middle school students.

Chapter 9

Experts Look at
the Middle School

THIS BOOK HAS repeatedly called for radical changes in the structure of schools designed for early adolescents. While advocating an interdisciplinary teaming approach as essential for effective instruction, the positions of Instructional Consultant and Coordinator of Independent Study and Student Research have been devised to help staff fulfill their new duties and responsibilities. Principals and guidance personnel have also been called upon to play different roles in the humanistic, personalized programs of the middle school. All of this is with one purpose in mind: to develop appropriate individualized instructional offerings that will enable emerging adolescents to become more and more independent in their own unique living and learning styles.

This concluding chapter will present the professional observations of five individuals who have worked in schools for early adolescents which have utilized many of the concepts and organizational schemes presented throughout this book. Each author has had considerable experience in middle schools and has worked with numerous districts on a consulting basis in helping them reorganize their operations to meet the needs of today's youth.

Eric Martinsen has been a middle school interdisciplinary team teacher. Vincent Hemmer was a Coordinator of Independent Study and Student Research. Raymond Stopper has served as an Instructional

Consultant in a middle school. Albert Cappalli is a middle school principal with a great interest in the area of pupil personnel services. Peter Telfer has been a middle school principal and a director of middle schools. Each of these educators makes unique observations which give further insight into different phases of the operations of an ungraded middle school.

––––––

A Teacher's View of Interdisciplinary Teaming
by Eric Martinsen

Mr. Martinsen was a member of an interdisciplinary team at the Liverpool Middle School, Liverpool, New York and served on the staff of Mt. Anthony Union High School, Bennington, Vermont. He is currently employed in the English Department of Connetquot High School, Bohemia, New York, where he is promoting an interdisciplinary approach on the high school level.

––––––

It can be safely said that the basic goal of all teachers is to satisfy the needs and interests of their students and, in doing so, create independent thinkers, learners, "doers." It is no secret that in order to satisfy this fundamental goal a teacher must individualize his approach as much as possible, and must utilize all of those motivational devices which will cause students to be open, receptive, and willing to take part in the lessons planned. A teacher must get to know his students well so that the necessary curriculum planning and student grouping can occur which will allow his programs to approach an individualization of those experiences he deems necessary for his students' development. He must also provide an environment in which the student wants to learn, an environment which in itself is a motivational device.

In order to do all of this, the teacher must be provided with a situation in which he can be as productive and creative as possible. He must be given a situation which makes it relatively easy for him to gather information about his students, and to discuss them with other teachers and guidance personnel. The teacher must have enough time and the aid of selected colleagues to develop effective, imaginative programs, meaningful to his students, in which subject areas complement one another rather than compete and conflict with one another. A curriculum and environment should be possible that, because of planned interrelations of subject areas, unencumbered by artificial, administratively scheduled periods of time, more closely approximates the life of the student. A structure that quite definitely satisfies these demands, indeed facilitates the program these demands suggest, is the interdisciplinary team approach.

The interdisciplinary team approach is defined as: two or more teachers from different subject areas, working together to plan for and teach a particular group of students. For example, a math teacher, a science teacher, an English teacher, and a social studies teacher would be given the responsibility of planning for and teaching a group of 100 students. All members of the team would focus upon the same 100 students. The team would be allocated a specific amount of time in which to meet with its students in its own assigned areas of the building.

Planning for the 100 students would include: grouping the students into sections which facilitate the achievement of goals the team has set for its youngsters; scheduling classes within the allotted amount of time; and planning a coordinated curriculum which concentrates upon interrelating aspects of each of the team's disciplines. The interrelated aspects of the curriculum might be skills, content, concepts, or a combination of these depending upon the emphasis determined by the members of the team. Creating a curriculum which interrelates aspects of all of the disciplines included on the team is one of the most important tasks of the team. The results of this effort help both to establish a more individualized program for the students concerned, and to establish that environment which in itself is a motivational device.

It is because of the possibility of interrelating subject areas that the total educational experience provided by the team for its students can be a closer approximation of the "life" of the student. Effort must be made to dispel the notion that "life" somehow only begins after a student graduates from high school. Life "is" always, at any time, and is not strictly divided into subjects that begin and end with a hoot, whistle, ring, or blast. Time, in the out-of-school life of the student, does not isolate, frame, or separate individual subject experiences. Time instead measures a series of overlapping, related experiences. Granted there are instances when the success of a particular experience depends upon some separate or individual consideration, and for the sake of clarity one must guard that experience from the intrusion of other experiences. But this resultant isolation is necessary and it is brought about by a need that is natural.

The experiences provided by the team within the school day must follow that same pattern. The team's plans should represent a totality. Separation or isolation of the parts that make up that whole should be motivated by special, individual needs, and not an artificial, inflexible schedule of periods imposed upon the school day that dictate when and how long English, math, art, or science should happen each and every day.

Care must be taken though that this suggested blend is motivated by the goals the team has set for its students. This blending must not be artificial, forced simply to satisfy the definition of the approach. There must always be purpose and reason for the coordination of the discipline areas. The resultant interrelated curriculum should be designed to best satisfy the needs and interests the team has diagnosed for its students.

There is a great deal of freedom in planning the curriculum in this approach. If the members of the team are willing to continually diagnose the students' progress, and are willing to continually develop experiences which keep up with and extend that progress, the freedom is limitless. The experiences, or more concretely, the units and related lessons provided by this potential of several minds working together, guided by the same purpose, can be both exciting and abundant, always extending beyond the horizon of any one single idea or approach.

It is impossible to state what team planning sessions or the resultant curriculums should look or sound like. The character of those sessions and the plans that result will be as varied as the teams and the students connected with each team. One thing that can be stated though is that each team must exhaust all possible areas containing information about the students on their team before designing the lessons with which the students are to be involved. Curriculum in this sense does not mean a year's work planned in September. General projections can be made to start the proverbial ball, in this case educational, rolling, but the individualized approach encouraged and facilitated by a team approach will cause that "educational ball" to roll in many different, fruitful directions. Control of that ball will only be maintained by continual changes in the curriculum experiences provided by the team for its students.

Some of the areas that provide information about the students include: student folders which contain diagnostic information, their interests, and backgrounds; guidance counselors who are familiar with the students; the teachers' own pretests to be given before a particular unit; and pupil conferences. When members of the team are satisfied that they are aware of the individual needs of the students, they then are ready to plan curriculum.

Not only is planning an interrelated curriculum most important but, as important things usually are, it is sometimes difficult and always requires a great deal of work and creativity. The following are just some suggested methods by which teachers can approach planning an interrelated curriculum:

1. During the first meeting of the team one member might suggest a specific area of his discipline as a possible starting point for certain students. The other team members then call out varied areas from their specific disciplines that overlap the topic initially mentioned. If, for example, the mathematics teacher led off by stating that an examination of a history of skills in math could prove to be interesting for many

youngsters, other possible suggestions from the rest of the team might include: the reading of math problems, the book or the film "The Dot and the Line," logic, statistics, math work in science experiments, math as language, symbolic process, map reading, and so on.

2. Team members should encourage the objective ideas and comments of their teammates in regard to possible units in each area. For example, an English teacher might be able to look at a particular math unit in a way not possible to the math teacher and come up with some relevant connectives between the two areas. The possibility of a dual presentation could be discussed.

3. Before determining the content of the team's efforts, the team might consider the following and design a program based upon its findings:

a. What are the students like? What are their interests? What are their home and family backgrounds?

b. What is the environment of their town or city?

c. What are some of the content needs of the students as related to their environment and experiences?

4. Each member of the team could bring in what he thinks would be an effective first unit of study in his area, and the entire team could then discuss possible overlaps of suggested areas. An Instructional Consultant or a party not a member of the team could sit in and offer objective suggestions.

5. The team could meet and, after a view of contemporary problems coupled with consideration of students' needs and interests, come up with a series of concepts that provide educational experiences relevant to the students.

6. Each member of the team, after a careful review of his subject area at whatever level applicable, would define those skills important to his subject area at that level. The members of the team would then meet to discuss the defined skills in each area to see if there are any skills important to more than one area. Units could then be planned which interrelate lessons for work upon these skills. The student who has some specific difficulty with English, but not math, might very well be able to get experience with a skill important in English in a math class.

Another important task of the interdisciplinary team is the grouping of students within the team. The grouping of students and the development of curriculum are dependent upon one another, and the effect that one has upon the other should make obvious the fact that, although these two tasks are discussed separately here, they happen almost simultaneously during team planning.

Grouping, as curriculum, should be created to satisfy the needs and interests of the students. It is because of this that grouping should be kept flexible. As certain needs are satisfied in a particular group or class structure, new groups or classes must be formed to satisfy needs not yet provided for. If a section of students has been created to satisfy a particular reading skill, when that reading skill has been attained, this section of students should be reassigned. This example is a simple, obvious one. However, when one considers two or more teachers of different subject areas working together, each with his own definition of worthwhile goals, the problem becomes more complex. Yet that need to continually regroup remains.

If the team, for example, is made up of four teachers, each from a different discipline, and these four teachers are given a three-hour block of time in which to meet with their 100 students, they must collectively determine the rationale to be used to group the 100 students. One teacher on the team might decide that he should meet with one particular group of students for a length of time that cuts into the length of time the remaining three teachers feel they should meet with different portions of that group of students. Conflicts arise. The importance of determining a satisfactory rationale for grouping becomes clear. This also points out the fact that the teachers involved must cooperate with one another, and each teacher must continually evaluate the goals he has established to justify his ideas for grouping to the other members of the team. All of this is to the advantage of the student because his program is continually being evaluated, not just by one of his teachers, but by two or more of his teachers, and not really just in terms of grouping, but in terms of curriculum and the realistic allotment of time. These three elements can never really be separated.

The actual teaching procedures for the teachers on the team can take many forms. Because there are two or more teachers scheduled back-to-back during a certain amount of time, it is possible for one teacher to hold a large class presentation while the other members of the team conduct several seminar group discussions. The variations of class style are limitless: medium groups, small groups, and large groups. Individual lessons could be team taught as well as team planned. There could be a large class presentation of "The Dot and The Line," a very imaginative film which introduces basic geometry. Follow-up discussion could be conducted by both the math teacher and the English teacher, with even further follow-up discussions in medium-size classes in which the math teacher builds upon the concepts presented in the film, while the English teacher discusses the film as a form of communication.

There are many advantages to the interdisciplinary team approach, but the greatest one is simply the fact that one teacher does not have to operate alone. The old cliche that two heads are better than one is beaten and worn, however it happens to be very true. If the team contains four members, there are always three teachers to help the one teacher having problems. Although a teacher has control and knowledge of the content of his discipline, it is entirely possible that he might not be able to come up with an approach that makes his subject effective and meaningful to his students. This teacher now has other colleagues to go to during the planning period they all share and ask for suggestions. On such a team there is not one but several creators, each with his own talents which can be sampled and shared by the other members of the team.

The evaluation of students and the solving of individual problems of students can be handled much more easily and effectively with the team approach. If the team is made up of four members, there are always four teachers to discuss the same student each teacher sees every day in a different context. If there are 100 students on the team, and 40 weeks to the school year, the team could arbitrarily decide to discuss ten students per week in depth. This would mean that every student on the team could be evaluated by four people at least four times a year. The resultant evaluation could not help but be more fair and complete because all four teachers could be focusing on the same student.

This continual concentrated effort to discuss students helps teachers to see each student as an individual. The teacher becomes open to the idea that because the student is an individual with unique needs and interests, he requires an individualized program. This understanding, coupled with the fact of the flexibility of his teammates in regard to curriculum planning and grouping, allows him to create an individualized program for the student.

The interdisciplinary team approach allows, and can almost force, a more careful, complete observance of student needs and progress. The interrelation of various disciplines permits the constant reinforcement of skills from one discipline to the next. The overlapping of aspects of one discipline into another shows those students who seem to be motivated by the content of one area only that there are things of interest in other disciplines. By being flexible with the grouping of students, by allocating time as needed and not as prescribed by artificial, inflexible time schedules, and by an imaginative, carefully thought out blending of the disciplines involved on the team, that motivational environment is created which makes learning easy and pleasant for the student because it more closely resembles life. And because of the continual meeting of the members of the team, questioning one another, justifying approaches and content choices, sharing ideas and strengths, a creative, more varied approach is encouraged for providing relevant, meaningful experiences for each student.

A Coordinator's Observations on Independent Study

by Vincent Hemmer

Mr. Hemmer was the first Coordinator of Independent Study and Student Research in the Liverpool Middle School. Currently pursuing a doctoral program in administration and supervision at Syracuse University, he is still employed in the same school.

Independent study is an essential component of any individualized instructional program. Not only does it allow for the development of a program based on the needs, interests, and abilities of the student, but it also helps to make him an independent learner.

During my first year as a teacher in the Liverpool Junior High School, I observed that several teachers successfully made use of independent study. Others, not understanding how to use it, misused it. Some were either reluctant or opposed to using this method. To rectify this situation, the position of Coordinator of Independent Study and Student Research was created when the junior high became a middle school. I was selected for the position. It was my job to develop and implement a program of independent study.

My first step was to learn as much as I could about independent study. I read all of the literature that I could find. I also interviewed people who had experience using this method. With this information, plus my own ideas, I began to develop the program. Two basic ideas guided my thinking. First, every teacher, whether he used my services or conducted his own independent study program, should use this method when it was appropriate. In order to prevent a recurrence of the problems of the preceding year, I requested that anyone using his own program keep me informed. Secondly, I did not want any student to be excluded from independent study merely because of limited abilities. Self-actualization of any individual in our changing society requires the ability to continually learn. This ability must be systematically developed. Independent study is one way of doing this.

Once I had developed the program, I turned my attention to implementing it. My first concern was with the teachers. Until they understood how I could help them, they would be reluctant to send their students to work with me. Therefore during the summer a memo was sent to all of the staff. It contained the rationale for the position, plus a tentative description of how the program would operate. During the August workshop, prior to the arrival of the students, I further discussed the program, answered questions, and solicited suggestions. That was my only meeting with the entire staff. The rest of the year I met with individuals and teams.

I scheduled regular meetings with resource teachers, content teams, and interdisciplinary teams. Although I had not anticipated it, my meetings with the content teams differed significantly from those with the interdisciplinary teams. Each member of the content team had completely different students. Since each teacher was urged to develop his instructional program based on the needs, interests, and abilities of his students, as well as on an interdisciplinary approach, there was little that the members of the content teams had in common. Most meetings therefore tended to focus on a theoretical discussion about independent study, or on relating stories about what their students had done while engaged in independent study. About the only benefit that could result from these meetings was a change in attitude towards independent study.

The interdisciplinary team meetings were in direct contrast to the content meetings. Here all of the teachers had the same students and were attempting to coordinate their approach to skill and concept development. This provided a concrete basis for discussion. Everyone agreed that these meetings were more productive and that the chance for attitudinal change was greater. Therefore, we decided to decrease the number of content team meetings and focus primarily on the interdisciplinary ones.

Independent study projects could be initiated in one of two ways. Based on the results of unit pretests, the teacher could identify those students who already had a grasp of the skills and concepts that were going to be developed. Keeping such students in the classroom would result in only minimal educational benefits. In such cases the teacher would assume the initiative and recommend that these students begin to develop an independent study project. By completing the proper form and submitting it to the teacher, the students could also take the first step towards developing a project.

Regardless of who initiated the project, the next step involved a conference between the student and the teacher. Here both content and skill objectives would be developed and clarified. I urged them to develop content objectives that would encourage divergent thinking. Open-ended questions or problem situations would force the student to choose from alternative theories or solutions. It could also result in the student proposing his own. Either way, he would have to defend his choice. The objectives were not necessarily related to those being developed in class. Finally, a time requirement consistent with the objectives would be agreed upon. If the student finished before the agreed upon time, he would report back to his teacher. If for good reasons more time was needed, it was granted. This prevented the frustration of not being able to finish because there was not sufficient time.

The next step was to notify me that the student would be beginning an independent study project. Before the student began, I would consult with his teacher and read his guidance folder. I wanted to learn as much as I could about his interests, abilities, and work habits.

After I had this information, a meeting was arranged between the student and me at which a number of things were discussed. We discussed the objectives of the project. We also considered the types of materials that he would need and how to use the library to locate them. I had access to the libraries in the community. Other agencies were most cooperative when their assistance was required. If technical questions arose which I was unable to answer, there were subject matter teachers always available in the Learning Centers. The student could consult with these teachers whenever it was necessary. Finally we discussed the daily summary sheet that he was required to complete. I emphasized the necessity of completing it in terms of how that day's activities related to his objectives. This gave both of us a sense of direction and progress. If I felt a problem was developing, I would make a note on the sheet telling the student to meet with me on the following day. The student could also request a conference if he wished.

Evaluation of the final report was an integral part of the program. When the student completed his project, he would submit it to me. I would go through the report writing down on a separate sheet of paper any questions I had. I would then forward the report to the teacher who would do the same thing. A conference would then be arranged which provided the student, his teacher, and me with an opportunity to discuss the project. The student was held responsible for whatever he included in the report. He was also responsible for things that should have been included but were not. The time required for these conferences depended upon the number of questions asked and the time necessary for answering them. It ranged from approximately 15 to 50 minutes. The average was about 25 minutes.

Students generally approached these conferences with a certain uneasiness. However, as the conference proceeded, most of the students developed a sense of confidence and accomplishment. After the conferences, teachers often mentioned how valuable they felt the experience had been for them as well as for the students. They expressed surprise at the maturity the students had displayed and the amount that they had learned.

At the end of the conferences each participant was required to independently evaluate the entire project, including the questioning. They were to be rated as excellent, good, fair, or poor. Our evaluations were then compared and a final rating was decided upon.

During the year 28 out of 34 teachers used independent study. While some relied on the program I had developed, others began to initiate their own. Some relied exclusively on their own methods. As a result of these combined efforts, over 37 percent of the students were engaged in one or more independent study projects.

The monthly total of students doing projects was:

Month	Coordinator's Program	Teachers' Programs
September	3	0
October	7	2
November	12	5
December	21	4
January	23	4
February	22	10
March	28	13
April	15	15
May	10	7
June	9	6
Total	150	66

These figures reveal two encouraging trends. First, the teachers showed a gradually increasing commitment to independent study. It was generally conceded that the decrease towards the end of the year was attributable to several factors. Many of the teachers wanted to devote some time summarizing the concepts and skills that had been developed throughout the course of the year. Others were afraid that the projects might take too long and not be finished before the end of the year. Secondly, there was a trend towards the teachers developing their own independent study programs. This self-reliance and diversity was encouraged. From the beginning, it was planned to phase out the Coordinator's position as the teachers began to use the method themselves. These people would then train new staff members.

Almost all subject areas were involved. In the program I directed the totals were:

Subject	Number of Students
Social Studies	44
Science	39
English	28
Mathematics	15
French	11
Spanish	8
Art	2
Physical Education	2
Industrial Arts	1
	150

It is apparent that most projects were related to the academic disciplines. In the cases of physical education, industrial arts, and art, the necessity of special equipment influenced the number of students sent to me. In such cases the responsibility for independent study rested much more with the teachers. Because of the problems associated with learning a foreign language, I expected few students. I was surprised at the response. Pretests showed that some students were more advanced than others. Therefore the teachers suggested independent study. The projects that these students usually did were to prepare work that they themselves would then teach to the rest of the class. They also tested the students on the material.

The time required to complete projects ranged from five to 30 class periods. The median was 12. The mean was 15. This does not include the time that the students spent on their own. Usually this was quite a lot, but no accurate record is available.

The quality of the work done by the students is encouraging. The final ratings were:

Rating	Percentage of Reports
Excellent	24
Good	53
Fair	21
Poor	2

The reliability of the students to accurately judge the quality of their own work was surprising to me. Approximately 60 percent of the time my evaluations and those of the students and teachers were unanimous. When the students' evaluations did not agree with ours, they tended to underestimate themselves. This occurred twice as frequently as did their overestimating their work. Only two projects resulted in total disagreement.

Student reaction to independent study was very favorable. All but two students stated that they profited from the experience and hoped to be able to participate again. The most frequently mentioned reasons for this reaction were:

1. I was able to go as fast as I could without waiting for the other students.
2. If I needed more time to understand something, I had it.
3. I was interested in the topic.
4. I liked seeing what I could do without having a teacher standing over me.
5. It will help me in the future.
6. I really learned how to use the library.

Based on the evidence, the first year of the independent study program was quite successful. The two basic objectives that I had established were both achieved to an extent. Many teachers used independent study and students of all ability levels had successfully completed projects. Independent study was thus becoming a viable method in establishing a nongraded program in our middle school.

A Guidance Program for Early Adolescents
by Albert Cappalli

Mr. Cappalli is principal of the Peconic Street Intermediate School in

Ronkonkoma, New York. His experience as a building principal, middle school consultant, classroom teacher, and president of the local teachers' association, enables him to perceptively comment on the role that guidance counselors must play in middle schools if they are to be effective.

You can't discuss the role and the function of the guidance department of a school until you have determined the philosophy of the school itself. Guidance counselors should not function independently of the rest of the school. Under traditional circumstances a counselor has a number of youngsters that he is responsible for and, in the course of a year, he somehow manages to meet his counselees on one, two, or possibly three occasions. At these meetings he attempts to be of assistance to the child. But in most instances the guidance counselor operates alone, although some attempt is made to get back to the teachers and involve them in the total situation.

Experience seems to indicate that, especially at the secondary level, the guidance counselor functions more or less independently of the rest of the school. Even if he were to attempt to incorporate his activities into the total picture, scheduling difficulties and the unavailability of teachers to meet with either parents or students at convenient times inhibit his achieving such a goal. The real tragedy of this is that the person who is capable of being of tremendous assistance in helping solve the kinds of problems the child faces in school, namely the teacher, is not truly involved.

Unless there is a certain amount of coordination among the counselors, the teachers, and the total school, the individual efforts of all the parties involved will go to waste. There are a number of interesting procedures along these lines being attempted in various parts of the country. I have been fortunate enough to observe a guidance-directed program in operation in my own school and happen to believe it is a reasonably effective one. It must however be recalled that the service that guidance provides to staff should be determined as the role is initially developed. As problems arise and as improvements have to be made, the role must be redefined.

The Peconic Street school houses approximately 700 students in grades five through eight. We have two guidance counselors, one male and one female. The school is committed to team teaching on an interdisciplinary basis. There is a conscious effort being made to involve all members of the faculty, regardless of their teaching area, with the guidance counselors in attempts to work for the best interests of the children. Realizing that if there is to be a dialogue between teachers and counselors, an opportunity to exchange vital information must be present, we therefore utilize block-type scheduling. This makes it possible to schedule teams of teachers for free periods of time in common with each other.

At the start of the school year these team planning periods are used for meetings of the building principal and the guidance counselor with the teachers assigned to the particular teams. These sessions are devoted to a discussion of the procedures that the teams will be operating under for the year as well as to an analysis of certain curricular goals that have been established. The meetings attempt to clearly define staff responsibilities. In the course of these discussions which are held on a weekly basis, the principal may become actively involved and may make certain requests of the staff.

We have found it to be quite effective to ask each team, after they have met their students at the beginning of the school year, to compile a list of ten students it believes will be academic problems and ten students who may prove to be discipline problems. This assignment is usually completed by the end of the second week of school. At the next meeting of the team with the building principal and the guidance counselor assigned to that team, this list is given to the counselor. It then becomes his responsibility to research the names and bring back information to the team that may be helpful to it, such as past problems of the student, contacts with parents, and teacher comments. Any information that can be presented to the team will be looked upon as a valuable service that has been rendered by the counselor. This will help to establish rapport between the counselor and his teams.

If after a series of meetings on these 20 students, a letter to a particular parent is deemed appropriate, it becomes the responsibility of the guidance counselor to send this to the parent. The letter should indicate that, after meeting with all the teachers and the principal, it was agreed that, in the best interests of the child, the parent should come to school and meet with the teachers. It is customary in my school to ask the male parent to meet on problems concerning his son, and the female parent to discuss her daughter's difficulties. The alternate parent or guardian will be accepted without a great deal of difficulty but, from past experience, the first way has proven to be much more effective.

The purpose of contacting the parent is to establish continuity of thought between the school and the parent, and to make the parent aware of the school and the responsibility that parent and school have to each other. If the child is to gain any measure of respect for both his parents and the school, there must be a working closeness between the two parties. The letter sent home is not a form letter. It is a personal letter directed and addressed to the parent. Upon receipt of it and telephone confirmation of a convenient meeting date and time, a conference is planned involving the teachers, the guidance counselor, and the principal, if his presence is needed or requested. The technique is then to meet the parent and have each teacher in turn present the nature of the difficulty as he sees it. A certain number of suggestions are made in the course of the discussion. At the conclusion of the conference four additional meetings are scheduled, each approximately two weeks apart, covering a period of two months.

Shortly after the meeting, or perhaps the very next day, the guidance counselor writes a letter to the parent. It highlights the major points of discussion at the previous meeting, calling specific attention to recommendations made by the teachers and agreed to by the parent. It requests the parent's support, calls attention to future conferences, and asks that the school be contacted at any time if there is a problem concerning the youngster. An important procedure to be followed as a result of this first meeting and follow-up letter is that all future meetings and contacts between the parent and the teachers must be arranged by the guidance counselor.

At this point the counselor should schedule a number of meetings with the child to see to it that the youngster manages to assume the responsibilities that are his. There are many ways in which the counseling services of the guidance person may be very helpful at this time. A child may be experiencing difficulty in planning his work or in coming to grips with the newness of the teaming situation. The role of the counselor at this time should be one of being a friend to the youngster and helping him see his responsibilities.

Where parents are uncooperative or where extreme difficulties seem to be evident, the principal of the building should enter the picture and actively participate in the proceedings. If there is no improvement after a number of conferences, and if the child still seems to demonstrate behavioral or academic patterns that are inconsistent with the team's norms for its students, a recommendation might be made to have the school psychologist included in the discussions. In many instances in our school following a number of meetings of parents and teachers, and a number of efforts to help the child, the school psychologist has become involved in the situation and things have worked out very well following an analysis of the problem from his point of view.

There are a number of good things which happen when teachers, parents, and guidance counselors sit together and discuss a child's activities at school and at home. There is the usual discussion about the behavioral aspects of the youngster. As one conference follows another and as parents and teachers begin to get to know each other, some very interesting things begin to occur. It soon becomes obvious that some time and thought has to be given to what one says when one meets with a parent. It becomes evident that teachers have to be able to demonstrate that they know what it is they expect of children. It is interesting to note that in this situation the role of the guidance counselor may be to assume a questioning point of view about curriculum. The questioning may be general in nature or it may be very, very specific.

Certain homework procedures have to be shared by all the members of a team. Testing patterns and grading similarities have to be agreed upon. A certain amount of coordination among the teachers on a team has to take place. The two basic questions that are continally being raised by the counselor are: "What is it that you are asking this child to do?" and "What is this child's capability?" In this situation the role of the guidance counselor becomes one almost of a devil's advocate. This is because it is the counselor's responsibility to see to it that procedures are adopted which benefit the child.

Since the counselor is in contact with several teams, there is a sharing of ideas and information from one team to another. I would also be quick to point out that in utilizing the team teaching approach to instruction, meetings with the guidance counselor and the building principal present an excellent opportunity for a certain amount of in-service training. It would seem to me that if it is important for teachers to participate actively and effectively in parental conferences, they must have in-service education in this area. By using the block-time scheduling mentioned earlier, teams are then able to meet with parents during the regular school day.

Observations of an Instructional Consultant

by Raymond F. Stopper, Jr.

Mr. Stopper has served as an Instructional Consultant in the Liverpool Middle School and as the Director of Secondary Education for the Liverpool Central School District, Liverpool, New York. A recipient of a doctoral fellowship at Syracuse University, he is currently serving as the Language Arts Coordinator for the Tredyffrin-Easttown School District, Berwyn, Pennsylvania.

Because the process of planning and implementing individualized instructional programs is complex and difficult, and because few teachers have experienced such programs in their own education or in their preparation for teaching, it is necessary for the middle school program to provide guidance for teachers who need to learn how to individualize their instruction.

The principal of course is the educational leader in the building. But in spite of his personal desires, his responsibility for the total program—including organization, administration, and relationships with district administrators, parents, students, and teachers—limits the amount of time he is free to work with teachers. In addition, the principal's role includes responsibility for the formal evaluation of the teacher's performance. Thus, in many cases, a teacher will hesitate to discuss problems which he feels might lower the principal's estimate of his ability.

District supervisors and coordinators are limited in the amount of time they can devote to helping individual teachers because of the numbers of teachers with whom they must deal. The "helping teacher" is also limited in the amount of time he can spend in working with teachers because his teaching load, usually including three or four classes, requires extensive planning if he is to do a superior job of individualizing his own instruction. It should also be understood that during the time he is teaching it is difficult, if not impossible, for the "helping teacher" to work directly with other teachers.

On the other hand, the Instructional Consultant's time and efforts are totally directed toward working with the teachers in one building. Because he has no teaching assignments, he is free at any time during the day to meet with teachers individually, to meet with teaching teams, to observe classes, to teach demonstration lessons, etc.

The Instructional Consultant has no authority. He writes no formal evaluation reports and at no time does he convey any negative information to the principal concerning an individual teacher. The latter is essential if teachers are to feel free to discuss any and all problems with him. Lacking the authority or the desire to impose change, the Instructional Consultant must use effective teaching methods in order to teach his teachers how to individualize their instruction.

The middle school organization described in this book provides maximum flexibility and possibilities for individualizing instruction. The Instructional Consultant can begin by helping teachers to perceive these possibilities and to test them in their daily instructional programs.

In helping teachers to learn how to individualize instruction, I found the following principles to be useful:

1. *Consider each teacher's interests, needs, skills, and experience.* Just as a teacher who is attempting to individualize his instruction considers each student's interests, needs, skills, and experience when

establishing goals and methods, the Instructional Consultant should consider each teacher's interests, needs, skills, and experience in helping him to learn how to individualize instruction. Teachers are at different levels of attitude, understanding, and implementation of individualized instruction. The Instructional Consultant will be, for example, working to develop the confidence of one teacher before he can begin to individualize his instruction, exploring with another the possibilities and values of using multiple texts, and demonstrating to still another how to use small groups effectively within his classes for different purposes.

If parents are unable to meet with teachers during the regular school day, the guidance counselor or the principal will assume the responsibility for the conference. Prior to the meeting teacher reports are forwarded to the person who will meet with the parent. After the conference the same follow-up procedures previously mentioned are employed. Again, every effort is made to indicate to the parent that there is coordination between teacher and guidance counselor. At the same time every effort is made by the counselor to utilize every bit of information the teachers may possess about the child.

A counselor review of report cards following the end of the marking period is another way of procuring potential candidates for parental conferences. It is customary in our building to review each marking period's report card grades. Any child failing one subject or working below his capacity will have a letter sent home requesting that one of his parents come to visit with us.

Having mentioned grades, it is always interesting to participate in discussions with teachers about various forms of reporting and grading. Needless to say, some continuity of grading is established by the utilization of the team planning approach.

It must be understood that counselors do not attempt to see every child assigned to them. They certainly don't avoid the possibility of meeting children on their teams, but they act primarily on the names that are provided to them either at meetings with teachers or through report card reviews. The interdisciplinary teaming approach allows staff to handle many matters that previously required the attention of counselors. But a child still may have a meeting with his counselor simply by either going to his office or by placing his name on an open appointment book in the guidance office. Since there is no pass system in effect in our building, students are free to move to the guidance office when they feel they would like to speak with their counselor.

It is also not expected that a counselor will deal with students that are emotionally disturbed. I question whether or not any guidance counselor has the training or the ability to deal with students who are emotionally disturbed. This is the school psychologist's responsibility in our building.

Thus the role of the guidance counselor in our intermediate school is to serve as a means of communication between teachers, parents, and students. There is constant review, highlighting important aspects of previous conferences. There are still a number of other duties that the counselor assumes that are in keeping with the traditional things that they have always done. They do, and I suppose will forever participate in, certain forms of scheduling and attempting to move students from one class or team to another. However with a team teaching situation and the teachers having more opportunities to group the children they share in common, the need for such grouping and scheduling by counselors is eliminated to a large extent. More time can then be spent in meaningful conferences with parents and teachers.

It seems to me that the approaches discussed here have tremendous benefits, especially in terms of the utilization of the counselor's time. Teachers feel, some for the first time, that they are getting a service from guidance; that guidance has something to offer them which they need. In return for this, they go to guidance with kinds of problems that, in the past, would often have been left unresolved. What you have in effect is a sharing of responsibility between teachers and counselors. Thus the role of the guidance counselor is greatly enhanced in this operational format. This is perhaps the reason why, in the course of one year, we had over 500 parental conferences.

2. *Teach teachers as you want them to teach their students.* Teachers are more willing to consider changing their approaches when the Instructional Consultant uses with them the practices he wishes his teachers to use with their students. In this way teachers are able to assess the effectiveness of techniques as applied to their own learning and, if successful, will be more willing to try the same practices with their students.

3. *"The more you try to individualize, the more ways you see of doing it."* This was the judgment made by Sandra Smith, a middle school teacher in Liverpool, New York. Teachers need to be assured that no one expects "instantly" individualized programs and that the ability to individualize will evolve with sustained effort.

4. *Individualized instruction is presently a goal, not an accomplished fact.* Teachers will be more willing to experiment with alternatives if they know they are part of the collective experimental effort by everyone connected with the middle school program—administrators, supervisors, guidance counselors, teachers—to learn how to individualize instruction efficiently and effectively. The day of the totally individualized program

has not arrived. The problems are complex and difficult. Teachers need to understand that the goal of a truly individualized program can only be achieved if each individual teacher makes his own unique contribution in learning how to individualize and shares his experience and works with others in resolving problems.

The process of planning and implementing individualized instructional programs is complex and difficult. In addition, few teachers have experienced such programs in their own learning or in their preparation for teaching. The Instructional Consultant therefore is vital to the development of the nongraded middle school since he is able to devote 100 percent of his time and efforts to the purpose of helping teachers to learn how to individualize their instruction.

The Role of the Middle School Principal
by Peter Telfer, Jr.

Mr. Telfer formerly served as principal of the famous Fox Lane Middle School in Mt. Kisco, New York, and as Director of Middle Schools for the Borward County Board of Public Instruction, Fort Lauderdale, Florida. A nationally known middle school consultant, he is now Assistant Superintendent for Instruction in Scotia, New York.

The middle school movement affords educators the opportunity to stand back and take a look at the total educational ladder K-12 and implement many changes that are long overdue.

There are a variety of reasons why a school district may decide to establish a middle school. Although some of these reasons may be economic in nature, there is a sound, educational basis for establishing a middle school program. The middle school has two decided advantages in bringing about change:

1. There is no tradition attached to the middle school, so innovation and change can be implemented much easier and quicker.
2. The staffing of a middle school necessitates the mixing of elementary-trained and secondary-trained teachers who will gain an identity of their own as middle school teachers.

The middle school movement has received criticism because people can point to many so-called middle schools and show that they have done nothing more than change grade levels without any significant changes in program. Unfortunately, this is true of many schools, but there have been numerous schools that have taken advantage of the reorganization by using it as an opportunity to introduce changes and improve the educational program for the pre- and early adolescent youngsters.

The key to establishing a middle school program with an identity of its own is the principal. Since the teachers function, in large part, according to what they believe to be the important functions the school is to serve, it is essential for the principal to communicate the school's philosophy, as well as its short-range and long-range objectives, to the staff. If he is uncertain about these areas, he cannot expect his staff to clearly understand the direction he expects the school to take.

The middle school principal, as a person, must have strong ego strength and be able to involve his staff in the decision-making process, but at the same time, let them know that he is the leader and has the final say for the total program. He must clearly indicate the kinds of decisions the staff can make by themselves and the kinds of decisions that should be discussed with him. In actuality, the staff will make its decisions within the framework of the program objectives that have been established for the school. One of the significant features of a true middle school is that the entire school must be committed to a program which will meet the needs of the pre- and early adolescent youngster. It must be made clear to all teachers that if they do not have this commitment, they should seek employment elsewhere.

The principal is primarily responsible for the selection of his staff and everyone knows it is the student-teacher relationship which really makes the difference. He must select people who clearly want to work with middle-school-aged youngsters and have an understanding of the nature of those youngsters. They should have enough self-confidence to be able to admit when they are wrong and to be able to confer with students about whether or not the program is meeting their needs. The middle school staff should have a proper balance of elementary-trained and secondary-trained teachers and a combination of experienced and inexperienced teachers. It is the responsibility of the principal to originally get this balance and then maintain it. He should make it clear in the beginning that the person is hired as a middle school teacher and not as an elementary teacher who will only have to teach sixth graders in a middle school program. If it is a team teaching situation, the teams should initially be composed of both elementary and secondary teachers. Once the teams are established, the principal should allow the other members of the team to be involved in the interviewing and selection of new team members when a vacancy occurs on their team.

The principal must set up an administrative organization which will support and enhance the instructional program. The question is often asked, "Who makes a better middle school principal, a former elementary principal or a former secondary principal?" This is a difficult question to answer, but it appears that the elementary principal's experience provides him with a good understanding of the middle school's philosophy and what it means to meet the individual needs of youngsters, but the mechanics of organization and scheduling are more like those of a secondary school. The secondary principal, on the other hand, must break away from the traditional secondary patterns of organization and provide more flexibility for the teachers and students. The principal should select administrative assistants who will provide strengths in areas where he is weak.

In a school of 1,000 or more students, the principal should have at least two assistants. One should have background and training in the area of curriculum. The other person should have experience in pupil personnel services. It is essential that the administrative title clearly indicate their major area of responsibility. There must be an overlapping of administrative responsibilities, but at the same time, the staff must understand what the special areas of responsibility are for each administrator.

The principal of a middle school must be an instructional leader who works closely with his staff. The administrative tasks which normally take up so much of his time should be delegated to secretaries, clerks, or business managers, in order to free him to work in the instructional program. Since the principal is the final authority in the school and is responsible for the teacher evaluations, he cannot expect his teachers to be totally open and honest with him about all of their problems. This is true of even the most democratic principals who actively involve their teachers in the decision-making process. Therefore, the curriculum assistant or assistant principal for curriculum, or whatever he is called, must establish a supportive threat-free relationship with the faculty in order to identify and work toward a solution of their problems. This person should not be formally involved in the process of teacher evaluation.

The administrator who coordinates pupil personnel services should have training and experience in guidance or a related field. The most apparent and significant change in a middle school, as opposed to the traditional junior high school, is that the school as a social institution is different. There is a friendly, warm, threat-free atmosphere and a learning environment is created where people care and try to meet the needs of the youngsters. In order to make this possible, all of the resources available to the student and teacher, such as guidance, psychological services, health services, social workers, and attendance personnel, must be coordinated and used effectively. There must be a different approach to handling discipline and student control. The emphasis must be on positive reinforcement. The person who coordinates pupil personnel services must constantly make the entire staff aware of the nature and needs of the middle school student.

The administrative team should schedule regular meetings with the teams of teachers. Team teaching is an effective method of organization in a middle school because if a teacher is able to function effectively as a member of a team, he must be flexible, able to give and receive constructive criticism, and willing to help others. This type of person usually relates very well to the students. A team teaching situation also means that problems must be faced openly and honestly, and hopefully resolved. They cannot be ignored. This is one of the reasons the administration should meet with the teams in order to bring the problems out in the open.

The schedule that is adopted is merely a framework within which the teachers can make choices and decisions. If it is important for the principal to know exactly where every student and teacher is at a given moment by merely referring to a schedule card, one cannot possibly have the flexibility which is essential to the success of the program. The true flexibility in the daily schedule will come about when the teachers can make decisions relative to the grouping patterns and time allocations for the various disciplines without having to get the approval of the administration or guidance counselors.

In order for the middle school to develop an identity of its own and to discard some of the educational practices which have not been in the best interest of the child, the principal must be willing to cope with many external pressures. He must communicate with the superintendent and board of education in order for them to understand the philosophy and objectives of the program. In order for him to gain the financial support that is necessary for materials and supplies, in-service education programs, curriculum development, and appropriate staffing, he must convince them of the value of the program. This means he must provide for the proper evaluation of the program with something more than just standardized test results. The parents must also be kept informed and educated about what is happening in the school and the lines of communication must be kept open. Parents should also be encouraged to visit the school to see the program in operation and informational types of meetings should be held frequently. The principal should involve his staff in these meetings.

The duties and responsibilities of a middle school principal are demanding. Whenever there is change, there is upset. If a person is willing to withstand the pressures and cope with the turmoil brought by change, he can develop a worthwhile and much needed educational program for the middle years. If the principal is not willing to do this and cannot provide the leadership and motivation, the middle school will become just old wine in new bottles.

Summary

The reflections of these five educators who have had direct experience in middle school programs attests to the unlimited potential of the movement. When competent teachers are given decision-making prerogatives and their efforts are supported by the members of the building leadership team, outstanding educational programs can be developed for early adolescents, thus assuring the middle school's success.

RECOMMENDED READINGS

Alexander, William M., *et al.*, *The Emergent Middle School*. Holt, Rinehart and Winston, Inc., New York, 1969.

Curtis, Thomas E., ed., *The Middle School*. The State University of New York at Albany, Center for Curriculum Research and Services, Albany, New York, 1968.

Eichhorn, Donald H., *The Middle School*. The Center for Applied Research in Education, New York, 1966.

Grooms, M. Ann, *Perspectives on the Middle School*. Charles E. Merrill Books, Inc., Columbus, Ohio, 1967.

Kindred, Leslie W., ed., *The Intermediate School*. Prentice-Hall, Inc., Englewood Cliffs, New Jersey, 1968.

McCarthy, Robert J., *How to Organize and Operate an Ungraded Middle School*. Prentice-Hall, Inc., Englewood Cliffs, New Jersey, 1967.

Murphy, Judith, *Middle Schools*. Educational Facilities Laboratories, New York, 1965.

Thelen, Herbert A., *Classroom Grouping for Teachability*. John Wiley & Sons, Inc., New York, 1967.

Vars, Gordon F., ed., *Common Learnings: Core and Interdisciplinary Team Approaches*. International Textbook Company, Scranton, Pennsylvania, 1969.

Index